Far Hori

Neale Edwards

PROLOGUE

The summer of twenty-twenty was to a great degree a busted flush. Just when you wanted to enjoy beautiful weather in the Spring, the dreaded Coronavirus had forced the whole population into retreat behind their own defensive positions. The barriers were up, all activity had ceased and the nation obediently settled down to sweat it out. Then a lovely summer came, and some relaxations accompanied this. But the threat, which was of nature and duration still unknown, had not gone away, and the current fear was of a resurgence. There was a faint hope that the warm weather might put paid to this awful plague, but there were no grounds for being optimistic about this, other than by reference to inflenza which it seems did withdraw before warm weather. There was no scientific evidence to support this hope though. As the year wore on, controls were gradually relaxed and life started to return to something like how it was before all this took root. But there were differences. People were reluctant to use public transport, go to cinemas, theatres, concert halls. They had also, in many cases discovered that working from home was generally a good idea. Think of the extra time you would have if you didn't have to commute for several hours every day. The appeal was obvious and it seemed likely to stick too. There was also the ever-present fear of a resurgence, a second peak, or even a third. Though there were instances like the re-shutting down of Leicester, generally the virus did not reappear in earnest and a summer of sorts was enjoyed, however restrained it had to be. Overseas travel was inevitably largely governed by the state of the pandemic in other countries, and the record was patchy. The result was that travel for business and for pleasure remained severely curtailed.

With the final act of leaving the EU, Great Britain had taken the plunge and left without the Europeans making any concessions. To have treated the UK as a defeated nation sparked up a strong reaction in even the calmest souls. The rest of the world, particularly the old Commonwealth countries and the anglophone world were generously supportive. After all, this

1

offered them opportunities as well, and they jumped at the chances they had been offered. In this climate, and following the experiences encountered during the lockdown in the advancement of electronic communication, this moment offered opportunity to those companies that could get ahead of the game and stay there in ways that would support and enhance efforts to expand into new markets. After the storm, there was an increased interest in supporting innovative and advanced small companies, and banks had appeared to have learned that they were fundamentally there to give support to growing companies, and not just to fill their own pockets with other people's money. Though the country had recently experienced one of the worst ever catastrophes, a silver lining glowed just the same, if initially somewhat weakly, and it would doubtless pay to look for it.

CHAPTER ONE

Derick Bilston was only five foot five inches tall. He was irretrievably unhappy about this but was resigned to the possible fact that this would not change, and he must pass through this life as what he firmly believed would be regarded as a midget. He felt that he was an outsider, which may have resulted from his diminutive stature, or it may have been because in relation to some of his acquaintances of similar age, he was indeed an outsider. Derick was just at the end of his fifteenth year, and a bright boy. He was as near useless at any sport as it is possible to be, and he had no regrets about this, save for a certain dismay over the lack of popularity to which it gave rise. He must clearly excel at something, and his active mind kept searching for this elusive quality.

He knew it must be there but what was it? He did find that he could tie most of his co-pupils up in knots in an argument, but he was careful about deploying this great virtue, because the likelihood was ever present that the discussion in hand would end in an unwarranted blow to his head. He didn't like being hurt, and it happened too often. This added substantially to his sense of not fitting in. On those fairly rare occasions when he found that he was interested in something which he was being taught, he concentrated hard and intelligently without difficulty. When the reverse occurred, he would pay almost no attention and would err on the disruptive side. This combination of characteristics did not greatly endear him to the teaching staff at Macclesfield Academy. In fact, the general opinion was that the place might be a lot better off without him. This was however, to ignore those moments of extreme concentration which most decidedly did occur from time to time.

Derick was utterly intrigued by the web and all forms of information technology, artificial intelligence, and robotics, and was a keen and well informed mathematician. These were subjects which strained the capabilities of most of the staff, therefore didn't get the attention which such topics required. However, Derick grew rapidly more and more absorbed by mathematics and its close association with the computer disciplines, so that by now he was something of a child prodigy and a budding expert. Once his interest was engaged, he learnt extremely quickly and thoroughly. Herein lay the skill and aptitude which he always knew must be there. He had now found it and was not about to let it go.

Derick lived in the back of Macclesfield, in a rather run-down part of the town. His father Stanley was a careful and unambitious man who worked as the mechanical brains cum foreman cum everything on the workshop side in a small engineering works which survived by being able to make pieces at very short notice for manufacturing machinery which had broken down and had thereby halted production. This was a small but fruitful market, because the effect of such a cessation in production was sufficiently prohibitive to warrant a good price for the services of C. Stevens Ltd., and a reliable support system for its seven employees. They were never short of work and their quality was high. Mr Stevens, Cecil, had invested modestly but shrewdly in modern computer numerically controlled plant, and his son Jason was the resident expert in programming these wonders.

Stan Bilston had first met Cecil Stevens when they had both been serving their apprenticeship at Rolls-Royce in Derby. Both were sons of engineers and were therefore accustomed from early childhood to things having to be right. There was no latitude between right and wrong in the eyes of their two fathers, who had worked on the aero engine side of Royce's in Derby many years before. The fathers had grown up in the glare of engineering perfection and had passed this view of life to their children. They had also found strings to pull at Royce's to get their sons onto the company apprentice scheme. This was a much-respected prize and highly regarded start for a young man. The knowledge and experience gained at Royce's would stand Stan and Cecil in good stead anywhere in the world where engineering flourished.

Cecil married a girl who worked in the accounts department at Rolls-Royce called Mary Milligan, and very soon they had their son Jason, while Stan eventually married Ethel, who came from his hometown of Macclesfield. The two men having discussed their future options over many a pint of Derby's best, and some late night mugs of coffee, decided that together they could and probably should set up a small high quality specialised machine shop in their native Macclesfield. Stan, the more cautious of the two did not want to be concerned with the business side of the proposed business, but he was enthusiastic about setting and maintaining engineering standards and running the machine shop. He just didn't want to get involved in selling and dealing with money. He had no ambition either to be the owner but felt strongly that he could find a thoroughly fulfilling and satisfying way of working by supporting Cecil in his new company. Ethel and Stan very soon had their only child, Derick, and together the two young men started what became Stevens's Engineering. They kept the original name for the first years, which was Schofield's Machine Shop, because there was already a business of that name which was well known, whose owner wished to retire, and for a very small annual payment the two newcomers took over his business. It had seemed a good idea to have a base load of work which had been done by the original company to provide financial cover while they developed their own business in rather more lucrative areas of activity. This proved to have been a good way to get the business going and the two of them became permanently good friends and colleagues. It bothered Stan not a jot that he was not a co-owner. Once the business was established, they changed its name to Stevens's. Stan always referred to Cecil as the Boss and the arrangement had worked well since its inception. Whilst Jason was interested in the business and had been trained in electronics and machine shop practice, Derick, who was a lot younger, showed no interest in things mechanical. His interests lay elsewhere in what would ultimately be highly technical and advanced electronics and information technology.

Derick's family's home was a mid-terrace house which had once served the silk and textile industries in their nineteenth century heyday. Their abode was in Newton Street, Macclesfield. It was now a small survivor of better times and provided housing for those of limited means. Derick's mother Ethel worked as a cleaner, looking after half a dozen small firms ranging from solicitors' offices to launderettes in which she was responsible for cleanliness and general tidiness. She was a proud and thorough worker and her home reflected this in so far as such a thing was possible. It wasn't easy to keep the place ship shape with a large husband who was dirty and oily when he returned from work every day, and a restless teenager who never tidied his room and left stuff all over the place.

There was no family car, but Stanley Bilston was and had always been a keen motorbike man. He had an Indian built Royal Enfield with a lightweight sidecar in which the family travelled on those rare occasions when opportunities arose. Derick had resolved that as soon as he could, he would have a car. He was embarrassed by the fact that his father could not afford one and was determined to correct this perceived slight as soon as possible.

Derick's family were Derbyshire through and through. Whilst Stanley's father had broken family tradition and been an apprentice at Rolls-Royce in Derby, his grandfather had been a keeper at a large pheasant and partridge shoot at Pot Shrigley. Ethel had rather luckily through a school friend's family found her way into the Macclesfield branch of one of the nation's prime department stores as a trainee shop assistant. Her father and mother had kept a small general store in Macclesfield, which no longer existed. Ethel's grandparents, the Sturmeys, had been the butler and housekeeper of a large grand country house on a vast estate in the middle of nowhere about ten miles out of Macclesfield, which, there being no family to inherit, had sunk into disrepair and had subsequently passed through the hands of a number of families with ambitions but no money. Its final fate had been as a boarded-up derelict, having failed first as a hotel, then as a conversion into flats which had never been completed, followed by a swan song as a failed care home. The carcase of this once magnificent creation was now known only as Old Dale Park.

Derick, on his weekend bicycle rides, would go up and ride around Old Dale Park and dream of the life which must have taken place there. His imagination filled in the huge gaps in his knowledge, but he was well prompted by what his mother had told him of the days when her grandparents had worked there for the Pitt-Curnow family. Sir Ralph Pitt-Curnow had been such a kind man in his mother's belief, and Lady Sylvia could do no wrong. On a special corner shelf in the sitting room in Newton Street there stood to this day a beautifully decorated but simple pale blue and white Chinese pot, which held pride of place. It had been given by Lady Sylvia when Sir Ralph died back in 1985, to the Sturmeys, because she was moving out of the big house into a much smaller one a half mile away. Lady Sylvia died very soon after the move. The Pitt-Curnow pot was treated with great care and reverence, legend having it that it could be worth a few tens, even perhaps hundreds, of pounds. The presence of this trophy was the main reason why the Bilstons didn't have a cat. They had seen on the Antiques Roadshow what a cat could do, albeit unwittingly.

Derick had on occasion gone with his father to see the Stevens works, but he was little interested in the mechanical side of things. He was bored by bell cranks and push rods, but the electronics under Jason Stevens's charge intrigued him. Derick managed to persuade Cecil Stevens to allow him to come to the works in the holidays and get taught by Jason about the CNC operations and the programming of the computers. Derick was only too happy to help out with such menial chores as the day's work demanded from time to time. For his schoolwork, he had a laptop computer, which had belonged to another boy who had sold it to Derick's parents when he had upgraded his machine. Derick had earlier been given another cast-off when he was ten years old, so he was not daunted by using such things. He only wished he could have something more up-to-date and more powerful. But that would come. He had been thinking, and he now felt sure he could devise a scheme whereby he sold something costing very little to his school fellows, in exchange for the possibility that the purchasing boy might win some sort of prize. He was thinking along the lines of a kind of lottery which would pay out some of the takings, but not all, so that he could make what was left over. He was aware that a scheme like that might never get off the ground, or if it did, it might not make a great deal of money. But something was better than nothing. And he wouldn't have to sweat for it like delivering newspapers for a pittance. On reflection, he thought most boys would be able to spend about one pound, maybe two, a week. If he could get say one hundred boys to join this scheme, and if he set the prize at for example ten quid, he would make between ninety and one hundred and eighty pounds a week. Something like that ought to work. Maybe the numbers would need to be massaged a bit, maybe not. Ten quid for one quid wasn't bad after all. And there were a hell of a lot more boys than one or two hundred. Suppose he could get four hundred to play this, that would start to make him serious money. His mind spread its tentacles into the remote corners of his fertile brain and ideas began to form. How about adding for example horses to this? Or almost anything that you could bet on. Football for example. He very sensibly wanted nothing to do with drugs. Dangerous, and you needed funding to buy your stock. No thanks, but just betting on all kinds of things had no buying cost, it could all be profit if you played your cards right. He thought a bit more and concluded that the way to get it off the ground was to be generous with the prizes from the start. That might reduce your profit, but it would give you a better chance of getting going. You could also employ some other boys to sell for you for a small fee. The same point applied, don't be too greedy, at this stage build the thing up. What was to stop him doing this outside the school eventually? Grown-ups had more money and lots of them liked a flutter.

Derick resolved to give his idea a go. Make the prize bigger to start with, you have to suck in your customers. And recruit a few people to sell, give them a small percentage of what they sell and see how it goes. It went.

After a term of this, doing one lottery a week, paying the prize on Friday so the winner had cash for the weekend, he started making a bob or two. It was working. He set his mind to having a sales force of five other boys, not more, and certainly he didn't want noisy extrovert boys. He was after the quiet considerate ones, the sort who liked maths and science, not the boisterous show-offs who you couldn't trust. Yes, five would be enough. Later he would direct this sales force to go for grown-ups at the weekend, but this was getting to the point where prizes might have to be both more numerous and bigger. He felt sure that there was a size and a market where he could make decent money without the whole thing getting out of hand. He made the simple assumption that the law would not be at all interested in his exploits, and that proved to be the case.

As fifteen morphed barely noticed into sixteen, Derick found that he was learning fast and well about the commercial computing world from Jason Stevens. Jason was not just interested in CNC and its connected computer technology. He was particularly keen to learn and to impart to Derick all he could about IT generally, as well as robotics and AI. Derick proved a fast and thorough learner; these subjects clearly suited his brain and he indulged in the subject as only a committed and driven boy can. He slept and dreamed about his newfound pleasure, he thought of little else. The money, not large sums, but enough to feel that he had done something worthwhile, allowed him to invest in an up-to-date and much more powerful computing system. He spent hours shut in his room. He studied learned books, he even joined a computer club in Macclesfield, The Second Macclesfield Probus Club, which occupied him for one evening every week. There he met members and instructors who took him to their hearts; they seemed to want to encourage and to help. This for Derick was a new experience. Gone was the boy who felt diminished by his size, who felt an outsider because of his dislike of games and of general rowdiness. He was accepted, liked, even. This was a new experience, and very heaven compared to school. Undeniably, school was tolerable and he still did quite well, but now he felt a real person and the beginnings of adulthood.

Then came coronavirus. The businesses that occupied his father and mother closed for the duration. School shut down. Derick was confined to the tiny space of the house in Newton Street, as were his parents. He was wise enough to know that it would help if he stayed out of the way for much of the time. This, however, was no hardship to him at all. He spent the entire day and much of the night at his powerful new computer. On the internet he found all kinds of instructional sites and drank to the lees all that he could cram into the glass of his mind. His knowledge grew apace, driven by that extraordinary stimulus, the teenage boy's mind once the dog had seen the rabbit. Had he been a musician he would have rivalled Mozart. Gradually it dawned on this boy wonder that there were opportunities within his new areas of interest. He had observed the way that the world in general had descended voraciously on computers and related activities to satisfy every need that could no longer be met by getting in the car and going shopping. He had marvelled at the rise of click and collect and the efficiency of Amazon. There must be many other areas where this new power could be harnessed to good and profitable effect. With the rise in working from home, he thought there must be an opportunity there. If you don't have to go to an office and can do things by electronic means without even getting dressed, there must be room for a service to enhance that new feature. Like a dating agency, there must be a need to match an employee in Penzance with a business in Newcastle, Neuchatel, or Nanking, and distance will no longer be the big limitation that it has hitherto been. He pondered day and night on this, and gradually it developed into other areas than employment. Many companies confined their customer area to a radius of a certain number of miles from their location. Derick having realised that distance need not now be any kind of barrier, also came to acknowledge that there were plenty of logistics firms and distributors who could take care of the physical side of all this. Better get thinking.

Eventually, though not until the autumn, schools got going again, but they remained hampered by having to observe distancing rules. Some had taken over new premises, others had done almost nothing, accepting the limitations imposed in the hope that normality would soon return. Derick's school did its best. It set up a temporary extension to its premises and called back retired teachers who were willing and able to be helpful. There weren't as many as the school had hoped for, but what they could find was a help. Meanwhile, Derick remained totally immersed in his exploration of all things computorial.

He started to think to himself that the world needed a business which he started to refer to as 'Far Horizons'. Once a mind like his is locked onto a subject, there is no dislodging it. French suffered, English suffered, Geography suffered. Computer Sciences flourished apace.

Christmas 2020 arrived and Derick got given a generous voucher. Stanley and Ethel were not brave or stupid enough to give him some computer gismo. They quite simply had no idea what he would like in that connection, only that he would get for himself what he couldn't possibly explain to his parents. They were loving caring parents and they had by now realised that they had an extraordinary son who had found his metier. They were anxious to support him in whatever way they could, but family finances precluded grand gestures. Initially Stan had made an effort to steer Derick towards the world in which he had found satisfaction, but he soon realised that such an endeavour would be completely wasted. He gave up any such attempts as soon as he realised that he had a son of prodigious ability in a direction which he completely failed to comprehend.

Derick found his mind wandering towards the subject of the country's imminent total independence from the EU. There must be a way in which a computer-based system could provide the framework of a hub to enable companies here to avoid having to do the donkey work of looking for new markets. It must make sense to use computer power to put all the information in one place so as to make a task which seems to be daunting, and therefore may never be attempted, into an easy reliable process. A sort of central system of opportunity, which entities in far flung places will be keen to join. Matching demand and supply over infinite distances cultures and languages is an onerous business. There must be something in this, even if, as they will be, others are concentrating on it too.

With the new year Derick was entering his GCSE year. He found himself wishing time would get a move on. His ideas of a business were already forming into something which he believed might fly, and he didn't want to delay more than he had to. This world of computers goes at supersonic speed, don't get left behind.

He would have a crack at his GCSEs, but the idea of Far Horizons had taken hold, and it didn't leave a lot of room for all this school stuff that he was finding less and less relevant. One thing was, however, certain. He would happily do Computer Studies and would walk the exam, since even in this short time, he had absorbed so much more than any school curriculum could cover. Derick felt that studying for that paper would in fact be a waste of time, because he was already streets past that stage. It was baby stuff to him, and besides, he had other larger fish to fry. But he would sit it anyway, what was there to lose?

Derick had started to think obsessively more and more about getting into business in one way or another. His great love and ambition was to set up in the computer world with his own network, hence the recurring presence of Far Horizons. He was convinced that there must be opportunities out there, and that it was such a fast-moving scene that he needed to get into it without delay. Things that other children talked about like University seemed to him to be no more than a distraction and a complete waste of time. What's more, Uni would be an expensive waste of time too. The bee in his bonnet was, to the exclusion of all else, his old friend Far Horizons which now filled all the available space in his head. The idea for it was forming more and more clearly in his mind, and he constantly reminded himself ad nauseam that he needed to be in a hurry to get on with it. Anything else would simply delay him so that he might miss the boat altogether, and he wouldn't let that happen if he could possibly prevent it. Derick had not yet noticed that this new addiction was beginning to worry his parents, who just did not understand how this could have happened. On one level they were proud of his prowess, on another they were scared that he might become unemployable and that his whole world could collapse before it had really got going. Parents think like that, but Derick had so far failed to consider that he might be causing the people who loved him more than anyone in the whole world to worry themselves into an early grave.

New ideas would come to him at the most extraordinary moments, sometimes causing great inconvenience to him and to others. On the lavatory seemed now to be a fruitful location, and often inspiration would arrive in a lesson. He carried a little hard backed A5 sized notebook in which he would jot down everything that occurred on these occasions. He would often wake in the middle of the night and have to get his notebook out and scribble a gem between its pages. It was getting very full.

Another tiny spark had recently begun to glow. Girls. He found them a great mystery, but he rather liked the idea of their company. However, he only entertained this thought at times of his own choosing, and he was very particular and unadventurous about this new development. He would take his time over this one, and when he had more time available for such frivolities, he would see about it. He was subconsciously scared that it might take up too much time, and he would most certainly not let some girl throw him off course with Horizons. He was aware that girls could do that, there were older boys at school who had been proper blokes once, but who now seemed just to moon about waiting for some silly girl looking like a Barbie doll to come by. He decided that if he ever made time to get to know one, she had better be brainy and know her stuff about computers. Nothing else would do, he could see that quite clearly.

CHAPTER TWO

It was a cold and wet weekend and Stanley couldn't get out to do any of the little chores that awaited his attention. Put more accurately, he simply didn't feel like it and so didn't do any of them. Not today. Stanley was not a great reader, but he picked up a recent tabloid newspaper that was still lying around and scanned it for some item of interest. There was none. He called to Ethel who was in the kitchen preparing Sunday lunch. This she always did, religiously. Sunday wouldn't be Sunday without a roast joint with Yorkshire pudding and roast potatoes. She couldn't make out what he was saying over the hissing noise of the joint being sealed in the frying pan before going into the gas oven for a full hour to make sure it wasn't pink. Stan always said he liked his dinner dead not walking around the plate, so she made sure that it was dead. Better to avoid arguments particularly when he was at a loose end and possibly a bit irritable.

If Ethel could have heard him she would have known that all he had said was where did she think young Derick was and what was he doing.

Derick was in his room, he hadn't bothered yet to wash or to dress. He was sitting on his bentwood chair, on his clothes which were still in a heap under him. He sat before his computer and was absorbed in some complex exercise which formed an integral but small part of his ambitious plans for Far Horizons. He knew what he wanted to achieve, but the method eluded him. He was sure there was a way through, but the light had not yet shone upon it. He was agitated, in a hurry, deeply absorbed. He was impatient because his sub-conscious could detect shiverings of a breakthrough, but his efforts still failed to tease out a result.

The uncarpeted stairs rang out as Stan mounted them slowly. He stopped outside the door and contemplated whether to go in or not. Derick might still be sound asleep, or as was nowadays more usual, he could be at his computer. Stan opened the door and went in.

"Well lad, what are you up to then?"

"Dad, shh… I am at a tricky point and I have to work it out, can you leave me alone please…"

Stan stayed silent and then turned and went quietly out, shutting the door behind him. He went into the kitchen where Ethel was quite clearly busy.

"Eth, I'm worried about that boy you know. All he does is…"

"Stan, I can't hear you over all this, can't you find something to do. Whatever it is, let's talk about it later."

"OK, Eth, I'm off to the Prince Albert for half an hour."

Ethel heard that. Half an hour my foot, more like an hour and a half, but I don't begrudge him that. Personally, I can't stand the place, it stinks of dirty old men and stale beer, and all they talk about is football or football. Not for me.

The Prince Albert was only a few doors down, further along Newton Street, over the little crossroads. It was very convenient, and really Stan was not a drinker, and he didn't gamble away the weekly wage. He was a good sort, it was just so bloody boring for him cooped up here with nothing to do but the occasional chore or some little repair to parts of the house. These were decently built houses. They may be small, but very little ever went wrong with them. There wasn't much that could go wrong when you came to think of it. They had been lucky to be able to buy the place, and that was only thanks to Stan having a good decently paid regular job. After all, he did have a skill, and that had pulled them through a time or two. Stevens's would be hard pressed if they lost him. He remembered when it occurred to him that he wasn't just the foreman, he and Cecil had started the thing and got it to where it was. Besides, he understood costings and estimating and had not dropped the firm into a mess ever. Not even once, and Cecil Stevens had been a friend now of many years' standing. Those two would occasionally go down to the Albert for a jar or two. It was good to have old friends, they were a bit of a rarity in the Bilston household, most people just got on with their lives and didn't bother each other much. Possibly they might help each other out with a packet of sugar or some small favour, but there was no real social life in the milieu of Newton Street.

Stan returned comfortably within the allotted half hour, as he had only had a half pint of Dragon IPA, one of the Phoenix

Brewery's specials which they brewed at Heywood near Rochdale. There had been none of the regular darts players who he regarded as pub friends there that morning, so it wasn't too hard to keep to the promised timing. If there had been, he would most likely have sunk a pint or two of one of their stronger brews like Black Bee Porter. Then he would almost certainly have been late, but he didn't like having too much at lunch time, because that blanked out the afternoon. On a day like this, though, blanking out the afternoon might have been the thing to do.

Stan was still worried about Derick, although he couldn't think of anything constructive that he could do about it. All Derick seemed to do was sit at that computer all day long doing God knew what. Stan's opinion was that he had better buckle down to his schoolwork and get a good result, because in life you needed a qualification. He was becoming increasingly concerned that his son was frittering away his time and might not be qualified for anything at all. He, Stan, had worked hard and got a good engineering grade, and an apprenticeship at Rolls-Royce, and had never been out of work. He had always held down a good responsible job and the family were even now the beneficiaries of that. No, Derick must wake up and start thinking about getting qualifications to secure the rest of his life. The rest of life is a long time if you are permanently worried about getting and keeping a good job, but he doesn't seem to understand that yet.

Stan walked slowly back to the house, turned the key in the door, and went into the sitting room into which the front door opened directly. The steep staircase was immediately facing the door, and it looked as though Derick's door was still shut. There was a delicious smell of a joint of beef cooking emanating from the small but well-arranged kitchen just off the main area. In the sitting room Ethel had pulled out the table and three wooden chairs and set three places for the ritual of Sunday lunch. She had taken off her red apron with the picture of a cow on it, folded it, and put it on the small kitchen table, ready to put on again when the meat was done. She spoke.

"Stan, what was it you wanted to talk to me about while I was cooking? I am sorry not to have been able to give you my full attention then, but the troops must be fed. What was it?"

16

"Well, I have been thinking. I am still a bit concerned about Derick really. He seems to spend so much time on that new computer of his and doesn't appear to do anything else. Like schoolwork for example."

"Oh, darling, he's only just sixteen. He'll come round to it, I'm sure."

"At sixteen I had already been working at lathes and milling machines for over a year and had been shown around the drawing office by then. I was at Rolls-Royce, remember? Maybe the drawing office was a little later, but my point is, I had already laid the foundations of a good respectable career by then. He has done nothing but play with that damned machine of his all the time."

"But Stan, modern jobs depend on things like computers, even at Stevens you have got CNC machines haven't you?"

"That's different, all they do is remember what you have told them and then get on with it."

"Well, that's what computers do too. But why don't you pick your moment and have a word with Derick if you're still so worried?"

"Oh, I hear his door. Yes, I'll do that."

Ethel raised her voice so Derick could hear her.

"I hope you're hungry, I've got a lovely hot lunch for you. Come on and sit down, and I'll bring it in."

Derick came rattling down the stairs and stood in the room, his mind obviously somewhere else.

"Come on darling, your lunch is ready. Sit down and I'll bring it in."

"Mum, can I be fairly quick please? I'm right on the brink of something important and I don't want it to go away, because if I lose track of it my whole programme will get lost. I find that stuff only stays in the brain as long as it wants to, and then it's gone, and you can't get it back. Well, sometimes you can, but mostly you can't."

"Yes darling, all right, but you must have a proper lunch, it's Sunday and I've done it specially."

Stan stayed silent. He would have liked to have said you'll bloody well stay here with us after your mother has taken so much trouble to make a special lunch for us. Like she says, it's

Sunday. But he simply buttoned his lip and said nothing. Too much of this forced silence could eventually cause an explosion. Stan liked to be the boss in his own house, and his worries about his son's priorities was genuine enough. For the moment he resolved to let it pass, he would pick his moment, but he must have a serious talk with Derick.

Mother and father made various noble attempts at general conversation, hoping that Derick might pick one of these subjects up and enter into a discussion, even a very small one. But the attempt was in vain, no more than the sound of bolting food and grunting emerged from their son. It was the sort of grunting that conveyed the clear meaning that he couldn't wait to get back to his computer and really couldn't be bothered with small talk. Even the mention of the China and Huawei topic failed to rouse the smallest interest, despite the fact that it was all about computers. Stan, who had served briefly in the Territorial Army, was concerned, when he thought about it, that China's intentions were almost certainly not honourable and would as likely as not cause this country some grief at some stage. Quite probably a great deal of grief and that could be quite soon. Thank God it now looked as if the plan to use the Chinese company had been shelved. Even he knew that the supply of the semiconductors that Huawei would need was substantially under American control, and that the availability of them could be cut off overnight. He had heard that the Chinese had, though, already stocked up with at least two years' worth of supplies of these things.

The moment arrived when Derick judged that he could now leave and get on with serious things back in his bedroom. He looked at his mother and father, both of whom he loved dearly, but whom he found it hard to understand. They seemed to him, as he grew older, to have different priorities from his own, different ways of seeing things too. He felt moved to speak kindly to them, express his gratitude and perhaps even also his love, but he thought better of it, and took himself silently back to his task, being unable to find suitable words.

He resumed his seat upon scrunched up underwear and a very dirty black tee shirt. Thank God for good broadband. He sat back and thought himself back to the point at which he had broken off for what he had to admit had been an excellent Sunday lunch. He must tell Mum when he sees her next, but right now, back to Far Horizons.

Derick thought to himself, this is getting so complicated that I ought to find someone who can help me a bit. Not some firecracker who will nick my ideas, but a person who will understand exactly what I am trying to do and can bring some expertise and knowledge to the table. It all seems to be a bit outside Jason's capabilities now. Above all, don't be shy about this, go and find the best, and if it doesn't work, get somebody else who is up to it. What I'd like to find is an older man who maybe has worked for Guzzle or somebody like that but doesn't want to set the world on fire. Guzzle had been founded in their apartment in San Francisco by Moses Silberstein and his girlfriend, later to be his wife, Esther Zhuvotkin, who regarded the name Guzzle as rather silly. Mo had simply said, it could eat any problem and that was its name. That remained its name and here it was now having grown exponentially, a world-beating top company. Most of that get-up-and-go kind, Derick had come to believe, do it on the backs of the quieter even cleverer ones, and that is what I must do. You can be determined, ruthless, and still a decent sort of a bloke. That may be hard, but it's what I've got to do. I won't ever carry any dead wood.

By now he had, he hoped temporarily, lost the plot. This was the moment to sit still, to concentrate, and go back over the morning's work and find the tags he could use to take him in the direction in which he wanted to go. This could mean a lot of sitting and thinking. He got up and went to his ancient mini fridge and took out a Red Bull, then settled down in front of his screen to puzzle out what had gone wrong. Damn, the drink had spat at his keyboard when he had pulled the ring. Handkerchief out and wipe it up. The trouble is, he reflected, going back over old stuff is so bloody boring. Never mind, that is what you have to do, that is how it works, and by the time you have got all this done, you will be dealing with millions upon millions of instructions, so you'd better get used to it. Actually that was a good illustration of why he wanted a dyed-in-the-wool left-brained genius, and what he wanted such a person to be willing to do. He must find that man, wouldn't it be good if there was one near here who wanted to have a bit of a change of emphasis in his life. Be on the qui vive. He made a mental note to put out some feelers with Jason and with the Second Macclesfield Probus Club next time he was there. He transcribed these thoughts onto his iPad.

As he was returning from his fridge again having extracted another Red Bull, he thought that the time could come when he would need a small place to work where he could store all the stuff that he would need if he succeeded in getting Far Horizons to move forward a bit. He wondered whether Cecil Stevens might give him a corner somewhere in his building. He seemed to have plenty of space, and Derick wouldn't need a lot of room. It would be handy too to have Jason available and in the same building. Jason was very useful as a second opinion, though his knowledge wasn't going to be the factor that propelled the new business out into the world. But all the same, Jason was a help in certain ways that Derick found beneficial. Yes, it would be good to have Jason around, even if all he could do was stop Derick from going mad.

This was all good blue sky stuff, and Derick was coming round to convincing himself that the whole school thing was probably a waste of time and that he might be better off just getting out now and concentrating full time on his plans, ultra-ambitious though they were. He was beginning to see this as the sensible thing to do, but he feared that his parents, particularly his father, would disapprove so strongly that a rift could quite easily occur. Maybe a talk with the teacher who taught computer studies might be a good idea. Get his reaction to Far Horizons. Surely there was no danger that he would go and steal a march on Derick's business plan. Then he thought again. Would Mr Blatchley understand it all? If he didn't he would hardly say so, but he would certainly pour cold water on the idea. Maybe this wasn't a good idea after all. On the other hand, he ought to understand it. That wasn't the difficult bit, it was the execution of it that would be so challenging. He decided to put that idea in the back of his mind and observe Mr Blatchley in action to form an opinion on this. Who knows, he may know somebody who otherwise I wouldn't know about. Yes, I might do that.

In the real world, as Easter approached, Derick had noticed on the media which he consulted regularly as a way of keeping himself up to speed on current affairs, that there was now a lot of talk and some impressive action on the part of business in general connected with getting into new markets. Having walked away at the end of last year from the negotiations with the EU over trade, the pressure was now on to develop links elsewhere and fast and under World Trade Organisation Rules. At least America was looking promising. It was largely for this purpose that Far Horizons had occupied and excited him for so long. This put added urgency into the mix, and Derick was more than ever convinced that the present circumstances created the opportunity for his baby and he had better go forward with all speed. The great advantage of the system he was working on was that it took the heavy lifting out of matching products to markets in every corner of the globe, taking account of all the relevant quirks, cultures, and conditions which stood to make the difference between mounting a successful export drive and getting nowhere.

As summer 2021 approached, the time to take the plunge got a lot nearer. By the greatest good fortune, he was beginning to hear of some quite impressive sounding potential associates, employees, or partners for the new enterprise. He felt confident that more would come out of the woodwork as he widened the range of his enquiries. Cecil Stevens had allowed him to occupy a small office on the first floor of his building, a couple of doors away from Jason's office, and Derick had wasted no time in getting installed. Thereafter he almost never left the place. He was seriously thinking that it would be better to cut school altogether from now on. It looked to him more and more like an unwarranted luxury which he could ill afford.

The time had now definitely arrived to confront the parents. He would steel himself to that task without further delay. This weekend would do just fine. The consequent dialogue was surprisingly brief and to the point.

"Dad and Mum, can I have your attention for a minute, there is something important I want to talk to you about."

Stan's immediate thought was, he's a homosexual, I always knew there was something odd about the boy.

Ethel thought to herself, poor boy is feeling unloved and wants a bit more attention. Well, I'm always getting at Stan to do more things with him, like a father should. You know, go fishing, do model aeroplanes, anything that would make him feel more included, more loved. I always thought that. Now look where we are. But this is what she said,

"Yes darling, of course. Stan, get a couple of beers for you two boys and I'll have a sweet sherry please. Now then, when your father's back, you must tell us what is troubling you."

Stan returned and handed round the drinks. It was very unusual to have a drink before lunch, even at the weekend. They weren't the kind of family that indulged together much in drink. Stan would go off and have a glass or two at the Albert, but otherwise drink didn't really figure in the Bilston household. Maybe at Christmas or on special occasions, but that was all. Derick cleared his throat and spoke.

"Mum and Dad, I wanted to tell you that I don't see the point of staying on at school after this term. I mean it would be pointless to go back in September, I already know far more than Mr Blatchley about my subject and there's not any point just sitting there when I already know so much about it."

Ethel, who was in reality not well informed about her son's strengths and weaknesses, interjected. As far as she was concerned Derick had no weaknesses and was a tower of undisclosed strengths.

"Darling, what is it that you know so much about?"

"Well, Mum. It's computers and all that sort of stuff. I am now pretty good at that and I love it. I have got some good ideas too, and that is what I want to talk to you about."

Stan breathed an inward sigh of relief at that.

"Go on, lad, tell us more."

"Well, it's like this. I know I have to stay at school until the end of this term, so it all fits in quite well. First, I don't want to waste any more time on A Levels next year, and I have already had a word with Mr Stevens and Jason and they will help."

Stan pondered this.

"You're ahead of me there, son, what did Mr Stevens say then?"

"You'll hear if you just let me go on a bit, Dad. I have worked out a scheme for a very useful computer search engine and I want to get it out there before somebody else does, so I talked it over with Jason, and he and I put it to his Dad."

"What did Mr Stevens say, then?"

"Like I said, he was impressed with it and said I could have a little office up on the first floor of his building at the back, a few doors down from Jason. For my computer and all the stuff I will need, I mean."

"Well, I don't know, he said nothing to me about this."

"He wouldn't, this next bit was only yesterday. He also said he would give me an unpaid apprenticeship so it would be legal for me not to go back to school. I also think Uni would be a great big waste of time and money doing basically nothing. Anyway, I can do far more in a week than those lazy people at Uni even dream of, so that's what I want to do. Well, it's actually what I'm going to do. That's what I wanted to tell you about."

Ethel and Stan looked at each other and each took a small sip of their as yet untouched drinks. Stan broke the silence.

"This is a bit of a how-de-do, I must say. And you were doing so well at school too. We've got to think about this Derick, that's what we must do. I understand, mind, how you probably feel, though. Personally, all I ever wanted was to get professionally qualified and do a good job, initially at Royce's, that I could be proud of. And I did that. Not much I can't do with a decent set of machine tools, even now, but I know we live in different times."

Ethel looked perplexed, then decided to row in behind Stan.

"This is all a bit beyond me, but like your father says, it is so important that I think we ought to go away and think this one through. I will say this. I admire your get-up-and-go, and if we can help, I am sure we will. That doesn't stop it all being a bit frightening though."

Derick was pleasantly surprised to find that his bombshell had been such a welcome damp squib. He didn't feel this was the moment to say any more, better let it settle and wait for Mum and Dad to bring it up again. He smiled to himself and went up the noisy wooden stairs to his room. His mind had already transposed itself into computer mode, and the beginnings of an important development had started to rumble in his brain. He sat down in front of his prized friend and started once more to revel in the intellectual warmth of the thing. Tap tap tap, he was away again with his innermost thoughts and pleasures.

CHAPTER THREE

Derick had put the word about that he wanted to meet senior people in the computer world, not just enthusiastic amateurs who might play with them as an earlier father might have played with Hornby 00 Gauge train sets. He had no idea where or how he might put himself in the way of the right person. He didn't even have a clear idea of exactly who or what kind of person might be the right one. He merely trusted his judgement that he would recognise such a person should one appear. Well, one had better appear, this task which he had set himself was demonstrating very clearly to him that it was one of those that would need several exceptional brains to crack it. This puzzle stood always somewhere near the front of his brain, but it did not prevent him from continuing to attack the near impossible by himself. If nothing else, he now understood only too clearly what the problem was, the hard bit was to make advances into the unknown on the way to solving this conundrum. He'd been at it now in Stevens's office for a good year, maybe more, he couldn't immediately remember, and what did it matter anyway? As long as he was going as fast as he could, he knew he was getting somewhere, but there was no doubting that the task remained harsh and tricky. By Sunday of this autumn weekend of 2022 he was thoroughly exhausted and felt like going on a bike ride to one of his old haunts which he hadn't visited for more than a year.

Derick got out his trusty rusty old bike, gave the chain a drink of oil, wiped the spiders' webs off, gave the saddle a good clean, and set off. His destination was Old Dale Park. He hadn't seen it for ages, but he still loved it, despite its sorry state.

He had forgotten just how far it was and was beginning to feel somewhat exhausted. He hadn't remembered that a good bit of the way was uphill too.

Nevertheless, after a bit of stand-up on the pedals, hard attacking riding, the great House started to show its beauty, far in the distance on a magnificent flat and level piece of parkland, at the end of a drive about half a mile or more long. He stopped, leant the old bike up against a roadside tree and gazed at Old Dale Park, with its lake in front and its massive pillars and vast number of finely proportioned windows. What a place, such a pity to see it neglected and becoming derelict. Imagine what it could tell you if it could speak. For once he allowed his mind to race in and out of imagined events and corners, enjoying the fun of letting his fertile mind momentarily off the leash.

As he drew up to the house, he noticed that there were a small number of people in ones and twos roaming about in front of the façade and towards the outer limits of the parkland. There were five or six cars parked in a haphazard way near the front. Among them he noticed a silver-grey left-hand drive Cabriolet Porsche 911. He admired the simplicity of its line and muttered, that would do me nicely. He then looked back at the house. So would that. He put his bike up against the side of the great entrance and decided to take a brief walk around and renew an old acquaintanceship. The other visitors were dressed in tatty dark nondescript-coloured ordinariness. How scruffy the English are, he thought. This place has seen better than that. Then he thought that's a bit rich coming from the likes of me.

After a quarter of an hour of wandering about the place, he thought it was high time he got going again. There were things to do. He turned and started walking back towards where he had put his bike, when he saw a figure rounding the far corner of the house, coming towards him, but still a good hundred yards away. This person was wearing a pair of emerald-green trousers, had a long pony tail of blond hair, and a leather jacket in bright red. He was wearing a fedora hat and dark glasses with emerald frames. Derick wondered what the dark glasses were for since the light had already started to go down. He soon came up to where his bike stood, and the man reached the Porsche and got in. Derick mounted his steed and pedalled off down the drive, only to be passed by the Porsche making a stupendous sound which gave Derick goose pimples. He thought, there's got to be more to life than Newton Street.

Much of the way home was downhill, and Derick was grateful for small mercies. It wasn't long before he was back in front of his computer at home. Given helpful advances in technology and the fact that Macclesfield was well served with up to date aids, his two machines, the one at home and the other at Stevens's could be treated as though they were one. Imagine how awful it would have been were that not so, as until recently had been the case. Thank God not anymore.

The rat in his mind ran round and round in its cage, unable to find the way out. Damn, it's a weekend. Bloody Sunday. Can I ring Peter Braithwaite from Probus? Just give him a nudge and tell him that I am still on the hunt for this amazing and unique man that I had briefed him about earlier. Surely he wouldn't mind. No sooner had the thought entered Derick's mind than he was on his smart-phone scrolling up Peter's home number.

"Hello?" A woman answered, so he asked to speak to Peter.

"I'm afraid he is not available, would it wait until Monday?"

No, it bloody well wouldn't.

"Well, it could I suppose, but it is rather important, do you think he might take my call? It's Derick, Derick Bilston, I won't be more than a couple of minutes."

"OK, I'll see if I can find him."

An unusually long pause for a very small house. I bet he was asleep over Countryfile.

"Derick, hello. What can I do for you?"

"Sorry to bother you on Sunday, but I just needed to remind you that I am looking urgently for someone to help with my project. Any luck yet Peter?"

"Ah, let me see. No, I don't think there is any news actually. We don't get many big shots at Probus, but I'll keep trying for you."

"Well, I just thought I would see if anything had come up. It is getting rather urgent now but thank you all the same."

"Wait a minute, there is a chap, very weird I think, but there is this chap who's come over here from California to retire. He's a computer whizz, I know that because a member who is in BAE Systems on defence computer work has met him and said something about him."

"Oh, Peter, could you please find out and let me know. Soon as possible please."

"OK old chap. 'Bye."

Weeks went by and nothing was heard. Eventually Derick could stand the silence no longer and he rang Peter again, this time in his office.

Peter came to the phone and said straight away,

"I'm so sorry, I spoke to this man, but he has now gone back to California to put his things in order. He has found a house in Prestbury, three miles out of Mac. I think it is the Old Rectory, anyway it is quite a substantial place and he will be back soon. I'll make sure that he gets to meet you, sorry to have failed to get him before. Oh, by the way, his name is Douglas Dominie. I feel there must be a story there. Bye".

Derick was overcome with impatience and had as a result been very irritable at home. The house was a very small place, and Stan and Ethel were reaching the point when they would like to see Derick living somewhere else. Somewhere else, but nevertheless very near. Stan wisely left the handling of this issue to the vastly more tactful Ethel. Stan and Ethel had discussed this at some length, much of the time going round in circles. They were also aware that Derick was clearly making progress and was looking for a senior player in his field to take things on to the next stage. They were also aware that time was rattling by and it was vitally important to get Derick's invention out in front of customers. His parents were at that point where more wealthy families would dip into their resources to give what help they could afford. Stan and Ethel could afford not a thing. Over the news at six o'clock, which neither listened to very studiously, Stan said to Ethel,

"You know that pot? The Chinese one Lady Sylvia gave the Sturmeys?"

"Of course I do, silly."

"Well, I nearly knocked it off its shelf this morning, I stumbled over the mat and put my hand out. Thank the Lord my hand only brushed the thing and rocked it a bit. I wouldn't know how to face you if I broke that".

"I should think not! Clumsy oaf!"

"Ah, but it made me think. You don't suppose it might be worth something do you? I think I remember being told that it was Chinese and very old. It could be quite valuable, and I heard on the Antiques Roadshow that the Chinese are now spending big money buying things back."

"I suppose it could be, a few hundred quid maybe, but it's only a crude looking pot my love, I wouldn't get too excited about it if I were you. Don't you dare knock it off onto the floor, it's got family value at least."

"No, I won't. I could fix a glass front on it so it couldn't get knocked. I might do that, I could make a decent looking job of it, and Adams down the road would cut the glass for me. I could frame it up and it will look a proper job when I have finished."

"Come on, time for our tea, I went down earlier and got fish from the Fry, and I've done the chips here in the deep fat, so they aren't going to be soggy. I know you don't like that, nor do I, so I've done them myself. I've only just put the fish in the oven on low, it won't be soggy either, so we should have it straight away."

The two of them settled down to a good plate full of cod and chips. Ethel had put it on a couple of white plates and they sat at the table to consume this feast. Stan mused,

"I feel really glad for our fishermen. Now they've got their waters back, we might have a proper fishing fleet again. It was always such a big thing all around the coast, then it went to nothing. I can remember as a child seeing pictures of Grimsby where Uncle Harry lived. It was so full of trawlers you could walk across the dock on their decks. Then as soon as Brussels got in on the act, it was all Bloody Russians and Frogs nabbing all the fish that were really ours, with trawlers the size of cruise ships. Thank God we've sorted that out. And a lot more. Good for that PM of ours, I say, even though he may look a bit of a mess."

As the fish and chips retreated gracefully into Stan and Ethel, the television ground on unobtrusively in the background. Derick had taken a curry which he had nipped out and bought half an hour before, up to his room. Neither parent could understand how he could sleep peacefully with the overpowering smell of a vindaloo in the room, but there was much about the young that they couldn't understand. Ethel cleared the table and put the flaps down to make more space, and they settled down in front of the screen. Stan was soon fast asleep, and Ethel went quietly to switch the thing off. She couldn't stand it being on all the time, and she was keen to get to grips with the new Jilly Cooper novel. A clever girl, that one.

In time for the ten o'clock news Stan woke up and put the set back on. A few minutes told him that there wasn't any more news and he didn't feel like hearing stuff he had already heard, all over again. He got up out of his armchair and gave Ethel a peck on the forehead as he passed her going towards the stairs and up to bed.

Ethel had a tidy up and dusted a few things that didn't need dusting and put away the plates and cutlery which by now had dried itself. Time for bed too.

Derick was quite capable of working on until the small hours, even until the small hours grew larger again. He was inexhaustible when it came to his all-consuming work.

He treated himself to a final Red Bull, and then threw his clothes around in a way that was almost contrived to annoy his parents. His grubby jeans landed on the empty basin, which he didn't bother to move, because now that bedtime had arrived, he wasn't willing to take up any more of the night washing. His underpants landed across the wastepaper basket which his mother emptied for him from time to time.

The now naked Derick lay in an abandoned pose across his bed like a dead body, and snored.

CHAPTER FOUR

Marina Slade-Knox was bored to tears. You have to have a massive bank balance to know that one of the by-products of such good fortune is the tendency that comes with it to have to endure times of extreme boredom. Marina had an enormous, barely countable bank balance. After excelling at Cheltenham Ladies' College at advanced mathematics, she had attended Trinity College Cambridge where her natural brilliance had been enhanced in leaps and bounds to the outer limits of that study. Marina also found time to engage in a bit of theatre with the Footlights. She discovered there that she had a gift for entertaining people of all kinds and that she enjoyed the business of promoting ideas, humour, bathos, anything at all, to an attentive public.

Cambridge had, to Marina, been a confusing experience. As a child she had not been interested in boys, and at Cambridge she found them shallow and uninteresting. They were either blokeish and played rugger and appeared to be vulgar brutes to her, or they rowed in boats going backwards and had little interest in anything but sex and booze. Boys simply didn't cut the mustard with her. She did, however find the unglamorous but hard working and generally quiet technicians to be worth knowing, but how could you actually go out with some of these miserable physical specimens? No, men were just not up to her standards, and to make matters worse, she had no real idea yet of what those standards might be.

By Christmas 2022 Marina had reached the point where she needed to be actively involved again with her fundamental underlying love for higher mathematics and problem solving. She had started life as a rich girl, her parents were extremely wealthy landowners thanks to earlier generations who had made fortunes from the cotton industry and from coal mining in Somerset around Radstock. She was indeed a lucky and well provided for girl. She had never wanted for anything, but her wants were anyway few and simple beyond her academic achievements.

It had been a natural progression for her to form a company with an American from Harvard, in the field in which they had both come to excel. She had met this man on her trip to America, the purpose of which was no more than to discover what made the place tick, but inevitably her interest was roused and she did more than just exist in this new environment. During her visit to San Francisco she met the amusing and effervescent young man with whom she would eventually set up a new business. The business arose out of a mutual interest in getting together to see what direction their energy and devotion might take them. Never did either of them imagine that the fruit of their exertions would grow and ripen as it had. And certainly they had no idea that it would get going so quickly. It started as a small part-time two-man shop, but very quickly became much more than that. Neither her new business partner nor Marina could tolerate the notion of part-time, soon their desire to get properly stuck in and make something of their imagined dream took precedence and the embryo of a serious company turned into a real viable being. This being became Chirrup, so named for the song of an extremely vociferous bird that perched outside their office window. It was never disclosed what was the species of this bird, it was just the inspiration behind the name they chose for their new company once it became a genuine serious entity. Luck was on their side, the tide of business development in the IT world was flowing in their direction and the new fledgling enterprise took off having been lifted by this piece of good fortune. Their success demanded that they get more support staff and one thing followed another so that their humbly born child became a full-blown adult business competing with the best. Her partner in this endeavour was a man called Douglas Dominie. Douglas was an extrovert with the technical application of a worker bee. He was supremely intelligent and had a capacity for concentration and sheer hard work that was unusual, so rare that Marina's admiration for his contribution was limitless, as was his for her. Rather surprisingly Douglas had rowed with considerable success for Harvard, performing well in their First crew at Henley Royal Regatta in England, winning the Grand Challenge Cup, the top award for racing eights. This did not count against him with Marina, she took him for what he was and also for what he wasn't.

Flamboyant in the extreme, it became apparent as success was visited upon them, that Douglas was also homosexual. Marina saw this as nothing but an advantage, for it removed the danger that the whole thing might turn into a romantic frolic and as a result fail to reach its potential. The business, which they had called Chirrup, progressed and flourished at the rate which only occurred when its underlying activity raced ahead, as does a surfer upon a breaker. The growing internet and social media revolution swept Chirrup along and the perspicacity of Marina and Douglas was of a sufficiently high order that they rode the wave with great skill and application.

Being rich and having nothing to do in the Valley made her turn her mind to reminiscence, in particular to the time when she first met Douglas. It had so happened that at a small and select meeting of the great and the good in the Valley, she had noticed a very odd-looking cove. Those who mattered most in this select gathering seemed to hang on his every word and give him an unusual amount of attention. Marina made up her mind that she should get to know this man. A few well-placed questions to her co-guests easily produced an introduction and soon she found herself opposite this wunderkind who was expecting to hear some wisdom from her. The other side of this coin had been that a bigwig in the room had sold him the idea of meeting this remarkable English girl. There was expectation on both sides, but for the instant both remained silent. Then they spoke together, the same words,

"What brings you here?"

This was followed by an enchanting smile from both sides and the introduction to each other by name.

"My name is Douglas Dominie. I know, it's a funny name. It was once French, but Ellis Island soon Americanised it. It was d'Ormigny, but that was too much for them, so they wrote down Dominie and it has stuck."

"I am Marina Slade-Knox. Don't say Slade knocks, everybody does."

These two unusual people circled each other amicably as do inquisitive dogs, then the serious business of who does what and who they were and where they thought they were going began.

The upshot of this was that they arranged to meet later on in the week to discuss the great question, quo vadis?

After they had parted and gone their separate ways, Marina got to thinking about Douglas. Longish foppish blond hair. Sky blue shoes, midnight blue socks. Matching pale blue jacket and trousers, pink silk shirt, no tie, dark glasses. Do I care? No I don't care, seems to go all right out here. Why not? His ideas sound good stuff too. I could probably help there. Must meet again. You only had to look at this man's sartorial efforts to see that he had an over-active mind, a strong gene of independence, and probably a need for a bit of help.

What she didn't know was that Douglas had retired to his penthouse in town and thought about Marina. Very upper-class English, but bright as they come. What does she do, I wonder? Could be just the one to help me get my bee out of my bonnet and flying, and get it all going bigtime. I bet she can charm birds out of trees, and tough as Hell I shouldn't wonder. She could twist the customers around her little finger and they would just thank her. I've got to get to know her. If she's as I think, bingo! If not, well, what have I lost?

A week later, Douglas and Marina had met in his penthouse for a proper heart-to-heart about the computer business in general and about his ideas in particular. A certain chemistry had begun to emerge as the meeting went on. Nothing sexual, she had already guessed Douglas might probably be homosexual, or that he could have some other strange Californian obsession which was none of her business. Whatever it was, it hadn't bothered Marina in the slightest. In fact, if it shut off a possible problem, so much the better. He was without doubt the cleverest thing on two legs she had ever met, and his opinion of her was not dissimilar.

After they had got together and formed their company which would eventually become Chirrup, they developed a system between them which was based on the ability to provide a comprehensive and sophisticated search engine which would enable customer companies to access markets which otherwise might not be capable of being found, particularly in the leisure and travel businesses. Marina thought it contained some very clever wrinkles and she enjoyed working her way through the algorithms and formulae that Douglas had devised and which he was prepared to show her. Douglas told her that he was at a point where his developments had now been proven and needed to be rolled out over a much larger market. It clearly needed somebody who was good at developing the market but understood perfectly what ingenuities lay behind the product. It became clear after four or five hours of deep discussion and exploration, that Marina could well be the answer to Douglas's prayer. The day ended on an up-beat note, and a glass or two of Bourbon, before they retired exhausted to their respective abodes and beds.

The follow-up, which occurred almost immediately after their meeting in Douglas's penthouse, was a visit to his tiny office. The young activity was on the first floor of a brand-new glass and chrome block in amongst some of the cleverest establishments in this world. There were a couple of interestingly dressed employees at desks who occasionally got up and went to filing cabinets looking busy. Because they were. Marina was pleased to note that they were women, and she doubted whether either of them was older than their mid-twenties or maybe their thirties. On asking Douglas about this make up of his people, he said there were a few part-timers who worked mostly from home, and there were some commission-only promotional people out in the field. It was plain to see, Marina thought, that there was a need to kick this thing into life beyond the office, and she warmed to the idea of taking the task on. By God, she would give it all she had if the chance arose.

The chance arose, Douglas immediately took her into the conference room and simply said,

"Welcome aboard! You will, won't you?"

Marina answered fair and square, no delay,

"Damn right I will! When do I start?"

So began a famously productive relationship. Salary was barely discussed, Douglas simply saying,

"How much do you want?"

Marina answered straightforwardly,

"As long as it has six noughts, I shall be happy."

CHAPTER FIVE

Given Marina's extraordinary ability to get into Chief Executive Officers' hideaways, and her ability to sell water to a thunder cloud, the Chirrup business grew at a phenomenal rate. It was plain to see that what Douglas and his team had developed did the job outstandingly well, and it also appeared clearly to be ahead of the competition. You couldn't count on staying in that position, but if you were first out of the trap you had a good chance of building a great business provided you didn't hang about.

It wasn't in Marina's nature to hang about, and results became apparent almost immediately. She was enjoying her new job enormously, and Douglas and she had sat down one evening and worked out the deal that they both thought would be equitable between the two of them. Douglas said,

"You know, if this thing really takes off, there will be so much bloody boodle around that I think the right thing for you and me is to go halves. I could never have done what you have done, and I have also to admit that you probably could have done what I have done. So, halves is fine with me, as long as we row in the most important of the staff when we have found them, to lock them in."

Douglas's idea was that they should split seventy-six percent of the equity fifty-fifty between them, thirty-eight percent each, and give the remaining twenty-four percent to the key employees that they must find without delay, probably about six or seven people.

Neither of them said it at this moment to each other, but the overwhelming thought behind this was to cast a super attractive fly over the nose of Guzzle. This was an active and lucrative market in which numbers were huge, anything could happen, and it could even happen fast. Seen from an acquirer's point of view, once he had assessed the prospective target, it would be better to pay well and get on with it before others got in on the act and before it just got bigger and the price went up.

This is the script that was followed, almost to the letter. Marina and Douglas sat in the penthouse room overlooking the beauty of San Francisco. Douglas spoke,

"Some you win, some you lose!"

"Yep! Fairyland!"

The growth and burgeoning of the little company was truly outstanding and beyond belief by traditional corporate standards, but the game had changed, things were now different, and the two principals were the beneficiaries in a way almost comparable to the rise of the Slade-Knoxes in cotton and coal all that time ago, but without the mess and the hassle of years gone by.

Chirrup had begun to make waves and become noticed in the marketplace. Important people in large multi-national firms saw the newcomer on their radar and they observed it diligently as it expanded ever further into their markets. This higher visibility led to Chirrup's receiving approaches from companies seeking to expand or shore up the areas in which the new arrival operated. Marina and Douglas resisted the temptations offered by these corporate wooings for a time. They believed that in order to get the best return they would need to grow a bit more to make the point that they were here to stay and were visibly a force to be reckoned with. This strategy worked. They were eventually approached for a third time by Guzzle, and a sale for an indescribably generous sum of money was completed. Marina and Douglas were now extremely rich young players and were both a known quantity in the Silicon Valley milieu. Douglas, as the business had prospered had become more and more extreme in his dress. He had grown a strawberry blond ponytail and he had taken to wearing odd mixtures of unusually bright colours. The true Douglas was emerging and he felt happier and more fulfilled to be able to present himself as he pleased, owing no allegiance to anybody else's judgement.

Since she and Douglas had sold out to Guzzle, she had felt the cold. She liked being involved and at the centre of things. She was good at that, and she must get going again somehow. Now she was faced with a potentially boring family Christmas which she must get through. Marina loved her parents and her family, she was devoted to them and bore a considerable burden of gratitude to them for the start that they had given her to her life.

It was just that not much happened at home, and none of them had any interest in intelligent conversation or in the arts, or in anything in particular. They lived a quiet well-heeled private life with no frills and no excitements. She was well aware that she was the odd one out and that her family occupied that privileged space for which others strive, some successfully, others dogged by failure.

Marina's father Desmond had led the cushioned life of a country gentleman. As a young man he had served in the Cavalry. After Sandhurst he had joined the Dettingen Dragoon Guards, the King's Own Black Horse. He had served in Germany at Bad Fallingbostel, first as a 2nd lieutenant Troop Leader in which role he was in charge of twenty five men and four main battle tanks ably assisted by a Troop Sergeant. After that he was promoted to the job of Assistant Adjutant as a full lieutenant before becoming Adjutant as a Captain. Desmond had made many life-long friends in his time in the Army and he thought of it as having been one of the happiest times of his life. Amongst the bachelor subalterns there had been much horse play and frivolity, although the Black Horse were highly regarded by higher command as one of the most reliable and best-led Regiments in the Royal Armoured Corps. As with all the Cavalry Regiments there was a highly developed esprit de corps which in dangerous battle conditions had on many occasions stood them in good stead. After leaving full-time career soldiering he had joined the Army Emergency Reserve in which he spent a fortnight each year back with his old friends. Though this was intended to be a serious training commitment, it generally also and predominantly became a holiday with good food and drink and the best of old friendships. Work got done, but it was not all that got done. Amongst the aspects that came under the heading of fun were trips to the Reperbahn in Hamburg where the most exotic and improbable examples of sexual invention could be witnessed. There were also many parties and Regimental Dances, and it was at one of these that Desmond met his future wife, Leonie. She had come out on the flight to Hannover for a rather grand ball as the girlfriend of a brother officer. Through the fortunate fact that this officer had found an exotic and attractive German girl from Walsrode, Leonie became briefly spare. At this point Desmond pounced in order to beat his fellow officers to the punch and grab the girl before it was too late. They were married and had since then enjoyed a wonderfully happy married life. The officer who had become bored with Leonie did not make a good marriage to his exciting German girlfriend. She soon tired of him and sought pastures new, eventually marrying the owner of a vast industrial empire in Dusseldorf.

When Desmond's father had died he retired from the Army in the rank of Captain in order to take over the running of the estate which as a result of his father's demise he had inherited. His life thereafter included much unpaid and charitable work, he was greatly admired by many in the vicinity of his elegant home, and he had been High Sherriff of the County. He had then become a Deputy Lieutenant. This was an honourable man who had given much of his time to the welfare of his home territory and his wife Leonie had been nothing but an energetic and loyal supporter to him. She had also been an outstanding mother. Marina was grateful to the Man Above for directing her towards the family that a benevolent fate had chosen for her. It was just that she felt no affinity for their way of life. That was all, and that had no adverse impact on her love of them.

Marina was back in England for good now and had bought a substantial country house herself, up in Derbyshire near Bollington close to Macclesfield, near where her colleague Douglas Dominie lived, and which she had grown to love. Somehow, she had grown disillusioned with America, fine for a visit, but to live there again no longer appealed to her. She had been intending to revisit San Francisco for this Christmas, but the earthquake the week before had put paid to that. It had been severe enough, but fortunately not as destructive as the one in 1906. Life goes on, but that had been a shock, nonetheless. People had got used to thinking it would never come back, but it had. Though Marina was entirely happy to be in beautiful rural Derbyshire, she needed something heavy-weight to do. Too much leisure she found disturbing, work being the only occupation that to her active mind was sufficiently rewarding.

Boys had still never been of great interest to Marina. She had found them generally boastful and rather stupid. They seemed to want to regale her with things about which she already knew far more than the offending man himself did. She had certainly never encountered a Mr Right, and had had the wisdom to avoid the crowd of Mr Wrongs who pursue rich attractive girls. Marina was attractive. Her hair was a natural and thick strawberry blonde, as it happened the same hue as Douglas's hair. She was tallish at five foot seven, slim, looked athletic, but wasn't, and was thoroughly articulate both in the English language and in the language of mathematics, to which by now had been added the full extent of computer science. She was a daunting prospect if you were just a run-of-the-mill quite attractive but not brilliant youth. When in New York she had made an attempt to see what this men-business was all about. Many of the men she had met were bankers or brokers from Wall Street, and she found that they could talk endlessly about finance but had practically no knowledge of the arts and culture in general. This she found tiresome as well as boring. Such interest as these paragons of the dollar were able to show in art centred on the value of whatever piece of treasure they might be discussing. She fumed inwardly and was silent outwardly. This would not do. However, she did feel that it was probably high time she learnt a bit more about what made men tick in general apart from money and no doubt sex. And this business of sex, what was so great about it? She had never found out for herself what that was all about, it simply didn't interest her, there was plenty of other stuff that occupied her mind and her body hadn't complained. But she was niggled by this and was aware that this sex thing seemed to suit most other people, so why not her? She was flummoxed as to how to go about discovering what lay behind all this, so eventually she tried an agency and got screwed a couple of times, but her opinion was that all that stuff was messy and vastly over-rated. Painful and undignified too. For the time being, she could do without it, and some women she knew had told her that she ought to try women, adding that they were much more reliable and knew exactly how the geography worked. That didn't appeal to her either and she didn't even bother to try to work something up in that direction. She concluded that if a Mr Right turned up one day, fine, but she was not going to go looking for one. Well, certainly not now.

She mused to herself once again on how she had gone on a trip to America some years back, and had visited San Francisco so that she could indulge in a tour d'horizon of that vast and varied country. Her natural inclinations had led her to Silicon Valley, where she finally felt at home and decided to settle for the time being. The idea was to see what might develop. She had more than enough money to enable her to choose for herself what to do and what not to do. What is more, she could keep this mode of life up for ever, thanks to her huge asset stash, should the need arise. At this stage she enjoyed the uncommitted freedom which that life gave her, and she revelled in the apparent competition among leaders in the field for her attentions. She was never confrontational or aggressive, there was no need for that. She had learned that such an approach yielded no dividends. She was, however, demanding. Very demanding intellectually. You didn't get away with waffle in her company, and if you erred into that territory, she would spin on her heel and be away without further ado.

Marina Slade-Knox had been noticed. Her waves had washed the shores in lofty places. She became the talk of high tables in the Valley and big shakers and movers competed quietly behind closed doors for her acquaintanceship. She met some of the weirdest people imaginable during her time in San Francisco, such a contrast to the upper-class English life with which she had also been familiar and in which she had been brought up. This was a long way from Cheltenham Ladies' College, and even from Trinity Cambridge.

CHAPTER SIX

Douglas was a happy man. He had never been a pauper, but he knew what it was like to have to be very careful with money. He knew that it was an extremely runny and thin liquid and would always find somewhere to leak from if left to its own devices. Douglas's father had been an aircraft designer with Boeing in Seattle and had earned a good salary for his work on the Stratocruiser airliner. This machine was a derivative of the B29 Superfortress bomber, the plane which had dropped the atom bombs on Japan and brought the Pacific war to a fortunate close, saving the lives of the many soldiers sailors and airmen who otherwise would have died in the conquest of Japan and its savage regime. His grandfather had come to America from France after the First War to seek his fortune. That he had never found, but he had built for himself a steady existence in motor engineering working as the head service officer for the local Packard distributor, also in Seattle. This work had been a far cry from the way of life enjoyed by his ancestors in France. That had been centred on huge estates in the Perigord Noir and the vast châteaux associated with them. His father's branch of the family had somehow managed to lose their not insignificant inheritance, and there was no prospect for Douglas's father to look forward to. He had simply been born into the wrong branch of the d'Ormigny family, and what use was it that technically he was a Comte? A pauper who is a Comte as well is just a joke, so he dropped all that when he came to Seattle. Besides, Ellis Island had turned his name into Dominie by then, so what the hell? Under his father's guidance, the family had never starved, even in the Great Depression, but the living had been hard. Douglas had been brought up to be responsible with money, and he had been fortunate to go to a first-class school in Seattle which had recognised his bent for mathematics and numeracy in general. This trend the school had fed, and Douglas eventually found himself at Harvard reading the most abstruse form of mathematics with great success and much enthusiasm. He had been a good and successful sportsman too when he went to

41

university. He rowed for Harvard at number seven in their first eight which won the Grand at Henley. To achieve this they had beaten Oxford University and Douglas was immensely proud of that fact, which explained why he wore a Leander tie rather more frequently than most. He was something of an all-rounder and generally of a happy disposition and endowed with infinite energy and commitment to whatever he chose to become involved in. He had many acquaintances, but few friends. He was a gregarious loner. Douglas was sufficiently resourceful not to need huge amounts of outside stimulus.

Having sold out his baby, Chirrup, he decided to move to England. Though he had sprung from French roots, he had little interest in settling there now. He spoke no French and he had no contact with the rich and smart branches of his family who still occupied high places in that country. Amongst them were ENARCs and POLYs galore. He yearned for the artistic qualities of Great Britain and he admired the country for its political and social stability. He felt that it was the true haven for a man with his achievements. He could live his own life in peace and without the attendant publicity of California. He didn't like the media and he didn't enjoy publicity. As a homosexual he wished to avoid the limelight and be allowed to conduct his life at whatever pace and in whatever way he may choose. He had found his ideal home in Derbyshire and was setting about making his house a true Heaven on Earth in his own way and according to his own lights. He also liked the fact that no one showed much interest in him, and he could dress however outrageously he chose, and no one would give a fig.

Douglas had always felt himself to be an outsider, he lived his life on the inside of his head, and there was always something buzzing around in his mind. He needed to be occupied and enjoyed facing up to problems and solving them.

While at school he had appeared to be quiet and ordinary, not showy or one to make an exhibition of himself. He dressed tidily in his school uniform without objecting to it and just got on with life, keeping himself out of harm's way and getting considerable enjoyment from playing with numbers. Though no star at school, he passed through the process well and in his chosen subject, extremely well, but that didn't make friends for you, you had to play ball games for that. He was no good at ball games. He had never rowed before going to Harvard, but rowing gave him his first real experience of public success.

After leaving Harvard, he had gone to San Francisco to seek his fortune. He had no idea how to do this and his father, though supportive, also had no notion of how the modern fast-moving computer world worked. He knew all there was to know about computer-aided design and manufacture from his Boeing experiences, but beyond that nothing. He made an attempt at persuading Douglas to go into Boeing, but it did not appeal to the lad. Douglas was set upon finding his own way, even though he had no knowledge of what that way might be.

Douglas just left home with the good wishes of his family and a small float of money generously provided by his father and launched himself upon an unyielding foreign world. He found cheap digs and set about working out what to do and how to find somewhere to do it.

Feeling momentarily low, he took himself to a gay bar one evening and met a young man there who had a job in Silicon Valley. They got talking and became friends, and Douglas eventually moved in with him. They had a partially successful relationship which lasted for about four or five months before the boy, Chuck Denver, lost interest in the sexual side of their relationship, but continued to be a friend. Chuck eventually found a fun-loving Italian boy who he wanted to move in with him, and Douglas moved out around the corner. The gay sex side of life did not so occupy Douglas's mind that he sought a replacement, rather he decided that he should be very selective about that and keep it entirely private and face up to the fact that there were probably many other things which were a lot better and more fulfilling than having messy sex with boys. This is the rule which in his later life he stuck to. But Douglas remained on very good terms with Chuck, and it was through this friendship that he gained his first exposure to the world that he would make his own.

While living in a tiny apartment on his own, he experimented with drawing and painting, but being of a self-critical nature, he drew the conclusion that his strengths lay elsewhere and gave up any embryonic ambitions that he may hitherto have harboured in

43

that direction. He did however decide that should he ever make it, he would collect paintings. He was irresistibly drawn to the late nineteenth and early twentieth century impressionist schools of painting. He greatly admired their way of making something magical out of what was ostensibly nothing. His particular interest and source of wonderment were the French Impressionists, the Concarneau school and the Newlyn artists. Though many other and different schools of painting gained his attention, those gems were his preferred study and pleasure. He resolved to keep his eyes on the auction houses in London New York and San Francisco in the coming years, though he knew he would not chase pictures as an investment and just to relish showing them to others in an effort to impress them. His interest was strictly his own affair and he would be extremely selective in anything he may acquire in the future.

Given the inevitable shortage of real money, he satisfied this desire by buying prints of such paintings as he admired, making sure that he bought copies which were as near as possible the same size as the originals, and framing them as though they indeed were the originals. This gave him enough satisfaction and pleasure to make it a harmlessly absorbing pursuit. Over his bed was a Renoir and on the bathroom wall a Monet.

He admired well-designed and well-engineered articles, be they wrist watches, clocks, or motor cars. He promised himself that if he managed to make a good bit of money one day, he would have a Porsche 911 cabriolet. He admired the way that Porsche had overcome the obvious handicap of putting the engine in the wrong place. There's nothing like setting yourself a totally unnecessary problem and then solving it elegantly. That is how he saw the Porsche car, why would you hang the engine out over the back? They had because they had originally lifted it lock stock and barrel from the Volkswagen, which they had also designed. For some obscure reason they had left it there, and the few attempts they had made to put it in the right place had gone unrewarded by a fickle buying public. That's business for you. And then they had ended up owning a majority of the share capital of the whole Volkswagen empire, and as a result, controlling it. Some achievement, that.

CHAPTER SEVEN

It was autumn 2022 and Derick was at home in the cramped quarters of Newton Street. He must find a set of rooms on his own where he could spread himself a bit and be his own master. Time to talk to the parents again. He knew he would soon have to start paying for a small office, and that he needed to get some help. That would all cost a fair bit, and he wondered whether his Mum and Dad could take out a mortgage to give him a start. That is if they haven't already got one around their necks. Does Dad make enough money to be able to afford one? I shall almost certainly need fifty thousand, and Mr Stevens and Jason said whatever you think you need, double it. Where was he going to get a hundred thousand smackers from? The bank? Waste of time and I would just be patronised by some old fool, that's no good. I don't know, but I'm going to have it out with Mum and Dad anyway.

Derick was in his room. It was early evening and he was still in his sleeping kit, which wasn't so different from his daytime kit, but the two were at least normally separate. He had come to a moment where he needed to sit and think things through before going further in his calculations. It was a weekend and there was nothing much to do, but that didn't worry him because the current problem was taxing his powers of invention more than usually severely. He heard the noise of hammering coming from below, interspersed with the odd grunt from his father. Obviously, there was some do-it-yourself going on. He knew this was not his father's strong point, even though he could work wonders with metal. Derick found it distracting and started to lose the thread of his work. He decided to get the rest of his clothes on, have a bit of a wash and brush his hair prior to going down to have the discussion about money with his parents. He discarded the dirty food-stained tee shirt for a white shirt. One he had had to wear at school actually, but it looked a bit smarter than his usual rags. Better make an effort and look OK for the parents, this is important. He opened the door and went as quietly as he could down the stairs. Even for someone of his small size, the steps were uncomfortably shallow and you had to go up and down with your feet sideways. It was made the more precarious by the fact that there was no handrail. He thought to himself, I must get out, this place is a nightmare for the three of us, I don't know how Mum and Dad cope with it. It'll be better for them when I am out, and don't forget that this is all they can afford, so just be grateful for what you have and don't moon after what you haven't got. One day I'll have it all, you'll see.

Stan looked up from his work.

"Hello, son, all right then?"

"Yes, Dad. What are you doing?"

"Well, I'll tell you. You see, I nearly knocked your mother's pot off the shelf onto the floor, and if I had there would have been hell to pay. It is her great treasure, and I do understand that, so I am putting a tidy little glass front on the shelf so it will be safe. That's what I am doing."

"Good idea."

Derick sat down and watched while his father tapped away and finally put the white painted frame over the glass.

"There, that'll please your mother. Well, I hope it will,"

Stan smiled and stood back to admire his handywork.

"Does it look straight to you? You know your mother has a terrible straight eye and I shall get socks if it isn't straight."

"Looks fine to me, Dad. Well done, that should fix it. Where is Mum?"

"She was here a moment ago, I expect she's just gone out the back, she'll be here in a moment."

Derick sat and bided his time. He chose not to say anything because there was nothing to say. There was a limit to what you could say about DIY, and it wasn't his interest or his metier. So he sat tight and waited for his mother's return.

"Oh, darling, thank you, that looks fine and it will do the trick. Is it quite straight do you think?"

A chorus of two,

"Yes, it's perfectly straight."

"Yes, I think it is. Well done darling."

Ethel went over to Derick and planted a small kiss on his forehead, then said,

"You're looking very smart, young man, to what do we owe this?"

"Well, Mum and Dad, I need to have a bit of a serious talk to you both. You see, I am at a point with my project, that's Far Horizons, where I think it is nearly ready to put on the market and try to do something with it. The trouble is, I don't think I can get it to the next and very crucial stage without a bit of money behind it. I'll have to get a proper office soon, and I am going to need a bit of help from somebody who knows what they are doing in my sort of business. I have got some ideas, but to make them happen I am going to need some money. About fifty or a hundred thousand pounds."

This presentation was met with a stunned silence. Both parents sat down and nobody spoke. Eventually Stan broke the silence,

"I think we all need a beer, and Eth, I'll get you a sweet sherry."

Stan left the room, principally to relieve the tension and give himself time to think. He hadn't the slightest idea of where a hundred thousand pounds could be found. And he had a mortgage, so that made things even more difficult. His final conclusion was that there was nobody else but the bank for that kind of money. He returned with a resigned reluctance to give his depressing verdict.

"My dear boy, I fully understand that you are onto something and that it is bound to need some money very soon. But I can't for the life of me see how we can help. You probably didn't know it, but I have a mortgage on this place and the spare value left over isn't as much as you say you'll need. I have no reason to disbelieve you, it takes a lot to get a business going, even I can see that."

Ethel sat silently listening and observing. She could think of nothing to add to this miserable story. Then she took her glass of sherry and sipped it in an exploratory way. Not too much, but enough to get the flavour of it. As she tipped the glass back, she saw the new DIY achievement, and a thought crossed her mind.

"I don't know if this might help, but do you really need so much money Derick? Would five or so thousand help you out at all?"

47

"Mum, anything would buy a bit of time, five would buy some, but I doubt whether it would buy enough. What had you in mind?"

"Well, I don't know, and I haven't talked it over with your father at all, so bear that in mind."

Stan looked at her quizzically. What on Earth could there possibly be that would give us even five thousand? He spoke,

"Eth, I don't know what you've got in mind, but we haven't got five thousand shillings let alone five thousand pounds. What are you thinking of?"

"I just had the thought a minute ago that the pot might fetch a few hundred pounds. Maybe more, you can't tell. The Antiques Roadshow says some things can make a bit, so I thought maybe the pot?"

"That's a family heirloom, from your Sturmey family and the Pitt-Curnows. You couldn't possibly let that go, could you?"

"Well, I could, yes, but it would be a big thing to do that. Though I can't think an ugly old thing like that would make anything more than a few hundreds, but I thought it might be worth a try. Just to find out."

"And I've just made a nice little place for it too!"

"Why don't we get that auctioneer to come and look at it? You never know."

"He wouldn't come down here to the likes of us, we'd have to take it to him. Just our luck to drop the damned thing, that would be."

This conversation, having made no concrete progress, morphed into a slightly stilted tea. Ethel had made a toad in the hole and some cabbage. There was fruit salad for afters too.

There was little to talk about, but a seed had been sown. Finally, at the end of the meal, Stan said,

"I will get in touch with the auctioneers in the morning, it's Monday tomorrow, so I'll borrow the phone at Stevens, and ring Adam Brandridge. We'll see what he says."

After a night in which all three of them built castles in the air, Stan set off for work. He chatted with Cecil Stevens and told him of Derick's problem. Cecil surprised Stan by saying,

"Oh yes, I know about that, Derick has talked to me about it. I think he may be onto something with his Far Horizons, but it is so damned hard to raise money for anything at all, and he won't get it off the ground if he can't somehow fund it. I would put a small amount in to help get him going, but I couldn't put my hands on real money, so that's not really much use. He can go on here for as long as he likes, but the business now needs some top people and the space to house them. A bit of professional marketing too. Well done him, I say, but I fear it is out of our league, yours and mine."

Stan rang the auctioneers and Mr Brandridge said he would be around at their house to take a look at this Chinese pot. Today was Monday, would Wednesday evening after work do?

Stan was surprised and delighted, it most certainly would do.

Stan, Ethel, and Derick had the greatest difficulty keeping their impatience at bay waiting for Wednesday evening to come around. Eventually it rumbled into view, and as good as his word, Mr Brandridge stood on the doorstep at six o'clock, an assistant with him.

The five of them sat around in the diminutive sitting room, and Ethel told the story of the provenance of the pot, while Stan unscrewed his carefully constructed show case and took the pot out very gingerly. He handed it to Adam Brandridge as though it were the Holy Grail. Mr Brandridge immediately looked underneath at the Chinese signature and the cartouche that incorporated it. He mumbled to his assistant,

"Yongzheng. Erm, interesting. Good condition too, no chips, no marks. Very unusual Mr and Mrs Bilston."

He turned it over and over and gazed at it from every angle, then handed it to his assistant with the words,

"What do you think Shaun?"

"I think it's pretty interesting, we must do some research."

Mr Brandridge cleared his throat in a well that's it for today gesture.

"Mr and Mrs Bilston, may we take this away with us, we both think it is sufficiently rare and interesting to merit a bit of research work back at the office. It is very old, it comes from the period between 1722 and 1735. Only a certain period of manufacture of a mere thirteen years. You don't see many of these because in that short time they made so few of them and they of course haven't all survived. And one in this condition is practically unheard of."

Stan spoke,

"Are you able to give us any idea of its value Mr Brandridge?"

"No I'm afraid I can't at the moment, but I can say it is going to be a valuable addition to somebody's collection. I will come back to you as soon as I can, but I would rather err on the side of caution and give you my opinion when I have completed my research into this unusually special piece. Thank you both, goodbye."

With that the two experts were gone. The door shut and the three family members stayed silent. Then Stan spoke again

"That very definitely calls for a drink. There could be the magic five thousand in that, or a good proportion of it."

Ethel spoke,

"I think you'll find that it is worth a few hundred when all is said and done. It's an ugly old thing and there isn't much to it is there? I mean if you had your cornflakes out of it you wouldn't give it another look. In the dishwasher and back on the shelf. We mustn't raise our hopes. Anyway, a few hundred always comes in handy. It won't be more, you mark my words and don't get all excited over nothing. But another drink would be nice, all the same."

Derick went upstairs and Googled Chinese pots. He put in the dates that he thought he remembered, and up came Yongzheng. Then he got back to his eternal task and forgot all about the plain old Chinese pot. Pots didn't tickle his interest in the smallest degree and this one failed therefore to make any impression on him. Besides, he thought it was an uninteresting and ugly old thing anyway. But you never knew. Pigs may fly.

It was a couple of days later that Mr Brandridge came back to the Bilstons. Could he come back and talk to them, would tomorrow evening do? And would they mind if he hung onto the pot for the time being so that it would be there for further research which may be necessary?

Mr Brandridge had rung the number at Stevens's and spoken to Stan, who confirmed that it would, and he could indeed hold onto the pot. Once again none of them could stop excitement from rising, despite their feeling that the pot was nothing really and should fetch maybe a few hundred. For them it had been above all a connection with family and Old Barn Park and the Pitt-Curnows, nothing more, but that was enough. It meant a lot to Ethel who remembered Lady Sylvia so well, and her kindness. She'd be sorry to see it go, they would have to get something else to go in Stan's lovely spot.

Mr Brandridge and Shaun his assistant were on the doorstep on the dot of six o'clock. Ethel let them in and thought she detected a little more respect from these two than they had witnessed before.

"Please come in and sit down. Please tell us what you think."

Mr Brandridge took his time, and then spoke.

"Not to beat about the bush, Mr and Mrs Bilston, you have got something extremely rare and unusual. Only a tiny number of these have survived, and there were very few in the first place. There is a considerable degree of interest in China now in buying back their own treasures, and your pot is indeed a treasure."

"Well, please go on, tell us more."

Mr Brandridge looked at Shaun, then back at the assembled family, then he spoke.

"Your pot is worth a very large sum of money. One like it three or four years ago was sold at auction to a Chinese collector for two hundred and twenty thousand pounds. Two hundred and twenty thousand. There was of course commission to pay on that, and normally we charge twenty percent plus VAT, but for important and extremely valuable items like this, we negotiate a lower commission. I am duty bound to say to you that you are not obliged, should you wish to sell it, to sell it at one of our auctions. It is sufficiently important a piece that you may need to take professional advice on that. Things like this only happen very rarely and I wouldn't want you to be less than happy with the result."

Stan answered him,

"Thank you, I am completely amazed by what you tell me, and I thank you for taking the trouble, and for your honesty in giving us the explanation that you have. We must think about what to do, meanwhile, would you be so kind as to look after it for us for the time being?"

"I should be honoured. If we uncover anything else, you will be the first to know. I can only assure you of our most professional service in this connection and tell you that we await your decision however it may go."

CHAPTER EIGHT

Derick was in his little office in the Stevens's building. He had been there an hour or two and was momentarily stuck. The numbers which he was juggling around his screen would not yield their secrets, and for the time being he was perplexed. He stopped and leant back in his chair, chewed the end of a biro and pondered his plight. He had been to his doctor for some minor ailment now forgotten, but he had been put on the scales by his GP, and he had also been made to take his shoes off and stand under the device for measuring his height. Joy of joys, he was now five foot seven inches tall. Maybe there was more to come? How gratifying.

He went out into the passage up to Jason's room. The door was open.

"Jase? You busy?"

"No, come on in. Coffee?"

"Yeah, I'd love one."

It wasn't that Derick was at a loose end, far from it, he just felt restless and frustrated. He thought a good way to get over this obstacle, whatever it was, might be to go and see Jason. He knew perfectly well that Jason wouldn't have a clue, and probably might even say so, but a leg-stretch would do him good, so he went.

Jason made out half-heartedly for a minute or two that he understood the problem and would think about it. Then he thought better of that and said,

"Just enjoy your coffee, then the answer will come to you. I know it will, it always does. Honestly, I haven't the slightest idea about that, you've left me miles behind, but thanks for asking!"

Derick could hear his mobile screaming away and he ran off back to his room and picked it up.

"Derick, Peter Braithwaite. You know the chap who I thought you ought to meet? Well, he's back, I saw him yesterday, we went and had a beer and I reminded him about you. He seemed keen to meet, so I want to give you his number."

"Ah, that's great."

Derick wrote down the number in his little A5 notebook, then put it into his mobile address book. He dialled the number.

"Hi, there. This is Douglas Dominie, can I help you at all?"

In for a penny, thought a somewhat nervous Derick.

"Hello, Mr Dominie, I am Derick Bilston, Peter Braithwaite told you about me, and I just wanted to have the chance to meet you and show you what I am trying to do." Derick paused briefly, "If you have the time?"

"My friend, I have the time. How would it be to meet at my place? Would this evening do? It suits me rather well as it happens, I should be delighted to see you at the Old Rectory at Prestbury at shall we say six o'clock? The house is quite a big red brick one standing back with iron gates and a long gravel drive, about a couple of hundred yards before you get to the Church, on the right coming from Mac. If you get to the old red telephone box on the same side, you've gone too far"

"Thank you, Mr Dominie, I will be there and look forward to meeting you."

"As do I."

The rest of the day was difficult. Derick couldn't get the excitement of meeting Mr Dominie out of his mind, and solutions to his immediate problem had been unusually elusive. He could see how the formula might go, and that it should work as was required, but the path from here to there remained obscure. He tried to stop being the terrier that he was and turned his mind to the matter of what he might say to Mr Dominie and what, if anything, he might expect to come out of it. He wavered from naked fear to extreme optimism and finally settled down, listening figuratively to the ticking of the clock. Soon it was time to go home and get cleaned up. Look decent, put on a tie, clean his shoes, make sure he had a clean handkerchief, brush his hair, and do his teeth. Mum was always going on about bad breath and how you mustn't ever have it.

Derick bestrode his familiar bike at five o'clock to cycle the mile and a half to Prestbury. He could always kill a bit of time the other end, but it wouldn't do to arrive hot and flustered and possibly late. He must get around to learning to drive one day, he would need to travel a bit more quickly soon, and go greater distances too, if all went as he hoped. It wasn't that he didn't like cars, he did, and longed for an Aston-Martin, but he didn't have either the time or the money, so there was no point wasting anguish over that. That was for later and he was as certain as such a young man can be that the time would surely come. Lots would happen, he felt certain of that. He passed the sign at the beginning of the village which proudly said Prestbury and found the drive on the right. Twenty minutes to go. What to do? He put the bike up against the wall by the gate and got out his folder with the stuff he thought he might need for the meeting. He sat on the bank under the wall and began going through the details that he had in front of him. He looked at his watch, still ten minutes to go. Just as he was putting his folder back into the saddle bag, a silver Cabriolet Porsche 911 slowed down and turned into the gate. It stopped in the gate and reversed a few feet back.

"Hey, you're not Derick by any chance, are you?"

Derick was a bit thrown by this, but he answered bravely and boldly,

"Yes I am, that's me."

"Hop in."

Derick took his bike inside the gate and propped it up against the hedge. They drove up to the door and got out of the car.

Derick realised that this was the very same man that he had seen at Old Dale Park that day. This time the man was wearing a light fawn suit with a pink woollen tie and pale fawn lightweight leather shoes. His socks were powder blue and his blond ponytail was made up in a man-bun at the back of his head to keep it out of the wind in the open car.

The two of them went into the house and up the grand staircase to a study at the back of the first floor. It was a good-sized room, but not huge. Derick thought you could get the whole of the Newton Street house in there with room to spare. It was extremely comfortable and seemed to have everything. There was a sound system, an array of computer gear, a large smart television set, home cinema equipment, and a very fancy looking piece of furniture that he guessed could possibly be a fridge in the corner; it had a wire coming out of it which went into a gold coloured socket in the wall. There was also a water pipe going into it. Funny what you notice at such moments. There were several leather button-backed wing chairs and an antique circular table in the middle, strewn with newspapers and magazines. At one side was an oval mahogany table with four exquisite wooden armchairs with leather drop seats. The walls were covered in beautiful and no doubt expensive oil paintings which Derick would love to have had the chance to inspect more closely. He thought one looked like a Renoir, it showed people enjoying themselves at a bar or somewhere, near a river.

Douglas Dominie steered Derick towards a deep burgundy leather wing chair, with side pockets which Derick noticed. Douglas then sat down opposite him in a similar chair in dark green leather.

"Now, young man, please tell me all about yourself and the clever system you have been working on."

Derick thought a bit before speaking and he picked up the folder which he had brought with him into the house. He didn't open it, he would only do that if Douglas wanted minute details, otherwise he had a good understanding of what he needed to say. He noticed that this Douglas was a good talker and had that undeniable quality that Americans can have, the ability to put one at one's ease. Derick now felt at his ease.

"Well, Mr Dominie, I think the best thing I can do is to start at the beginning and take you through the development of Far Horizons, and then bring you up to date on where it is now. If it is all too simple, hurry me up, I won't be offended, I just want to make sure that I give you a clear picture of my work without boring you."

"If I may, I'll call you Derick, and would you please call me Douglas? I shan't be bored, but I do have a good idea of what you are up to, and what I've heard I like. Please go on."

Derick set to and covered the subject in an organised and logical order. Douglas listened intently, sitting forward in his chair. This man was obviously intrigued by what Derick had done and wanted to know as much as possible about it. Finally, Douglas spoke.

"Are you telling me you did all this yourself. No help, nobody else involved?"

"Well, yes, I am really. I have had a bit of moral support from Jason at work, he's the son of my father's boss, but he really only knows about CNC workshop machinery. Jason is a good man to have for those moments when the brain needs a rest."

"I am speechless. I really don't know what to say. This is miraculous stuff, I can hardly believe you have created all this on your own, but you quite clearly have. Peter Braithwaite was right. Good old Peter."

"Oh, thank you Douglas, I am so pleased that you think it is quite good, that is the best thing I have ever heard. Thank you again,"

"Derick, do you think you and I could spend a bit of time, perhaps in your office, going through some of the detail? I see you have a folder there, is it for me? I would so much like to see anything that you feel you can show me."

Then, as an afterthought,

"Well, right now, what's the point of holding back? I am very interested and feel impatient to know more."

Derick held out the folder and passed it to Douglas.

"Here you are, help yourself. Yes please, if you came to Stevens's to my office, I could show you everything and I would be so pleased to do that. Just say when you want to come."

Douglas got up and picked up his smart mobile.

"Let's see what days are available. Go on, let's do it tomorrow, Vladimir Putin can wait!"

"Good God!"

"No, just joking! Would tomorrow morning suit you?"

"Oh, yes, it certainly would, you have the address, don't you?"

"I do. See you at nine o'clock then. I must tell you, I have some ideas that I think might make this fly. I won't go into them now, but I will run it all past you just as soon as I have sorted my thoughts out."

"That sounds wonderful, I can't wait to hear your thoughts and ideas."

"One thing I want to get out on the table, and then we can forget about it. I am a queer. That means that if I like anything, I like boys, but I want you to know that never will you be in any danger. And never will I embarrass you."

57

"I can cope with that, it doesn't have to concern us I don't think. I'm one ahead of you, I don't like boys and I think most girls are a waste of space, so there."

"You will have noticed that I look a bit different. I like colour and don't see why the girls should have it all. See this pink tie? You won't believe it, but it's English. Good old ultra-traditional English. When I was at Harvard, I rowed for them at Henley and we won the Grand. I got made a member of the most prestigious rowing club in the world, Leander Club at Henley. This is their tie and at the Regatta you see lots of crusty old men wearing it. And me!"

"I like that Douglas. Life need never be boring!"

Derick left and got on his bike. If he could have sung he would have, but his opinion was that he didn't have much of a voice so he had better shut up. He bellowed to himself inside his head until he got back to the squalid contrast of Newton Street. His mother and father were watching the television when he came in. Ethel got up and switched it off.

"Darling, how did you get on?"

"Well, he's a queer, but I liked him and I'm not scared by that. He put this fact straight on the table and told me I would be in no danger ever. And I believed him. I still believe him. I think there might be an opportunity here, I'm dog-tired now, but I will tell you soon. He is coming to Stevens's tomorrow morning at nine o'clock to see the details of my stuff. He seems very impressed and can't believe that I have done it all myself. Or that is what he says."

Stan spoke,

"Thanks for telling me that, son. It's a different world now I suppose, I don't know, but you're a sensible chap, let's see where all this takes us, I say. It sounds exciting, well done, you never know."

Back at the Old Rectory Douglas rang his close friend and colleague Marina Slade-Knox, with whom he had built up Chirrup before selling it to Guzzle. He felt very fortunate that the two of them had now settled in this heavenly part of the world. Each was a bit of a loner and they must have drifted together as a result, and by chance when Douglas had been looking for his house, another had come up, and he just happened to tell Marina about it. That was how it had happened and both of them were so far pleased with the result. It was good to have an old friend nearby, while still being far enough away to be completely independent. It had worked well.

The telephone rang in Marina's drawing room, and she answered it immediately, then Douglas spoke.

"Are you bored?"

"Oh, Douglas, what's this about? Actually, yes I am, bored to bloody tears. Come on then, spill it."

"If you're bored, come around and I'll get a couple of pizzas. I'll put some Veuve Clicquot in the fridge since it's you."

"I'll be there, just throw on some clothes. See you."

A very short time later, a sage green Bentley Continental GT drew up outside the Old Rectory, uttering a sound like a dozen French horns, and Marina got out. She had parked it alongside the Porsche Cabriolet having turned it first so that it faced out. Daddy had taught her this in case she had to make a quick get-away should the need ever arise. Not for nothing had Daddy been an old Cavalryman and wise in such matters. She was wearing shape-hugging black velvet trousers, around her slim waist was a fine gold chain belt. Her earrings were a significant pair of diamonds mounted in gold. At the neck she wore a thin gold chain with a Tiffany gold cross. Over her shapely top half was an open-necked brick-red linen shirt with small brass buttons like signet rings, decorated with the Slade-Knox crest. She knew Douglas would notice that and would appreciate it. The buttons had been a present to herself at Christmas last year, but she didn't wear this shirt much. She was very fond of it, particularly the buttons with the fox's mask above a barrel insignia. She imagined that the fox must have had something to do with the fox-hunting Exmoor Slades to whom she was supposed to be distantly related. She had no idea where the barrel came from but was quite happy to have that reminder of the good life. Knox being good whisky drinking Scots, it probably came from them. On her right wrist was an exquisite Vacheron Constant ultra-thin clear-faced white-gold watch, a prized possession which she was never without, and on her wedding finger was a brightly glistening large diamond cluster ring. This latter she wore to ward off unwanted attention, a hazard she had by now become accustomed to, but had never enjoyed. She was impatient and intolerant, and disparaging about most men. Nothing remotely interesting had passed her way up until now, and she was unconcerned, relieved even, about this state of affairs. This evening however might be fun, Douglas was always good for a laugh, and intellectually he punched her weight with apparent ease. And anyway he was a committed though probably inactive queer, so that was all right.

Marina had let herself in and gone up to the first-floor study where she knew she would find him. Douglas greeted her,

"Come in, my Muse."

He was attired in a midnight blue smoking jacket with gold frogging, over turquoise silk trousers, and an open off-white silk shirt. He had velvet slippers on his feet with DD embroidered in gold thread on each. He had ordered them from Lobb's and told them that the DD must be an exact copy of the DD logo for Double Diamond beer. Invisibly, Mr Lobb had raised an eyebrow and complied.

A silent manservant glided into the room and put two hot pizzas on the table, then glided out again. Douglas took the Widow from the fridge in the corner, opened it without a pop, and poured two glasses, handing one to Marina. They smiled and clicked their glasses, then sat opposite each other in a pair of leather wing chairs. The pizzas would have to wait until they got up again and sank into a pair of Chippendale original armchairs to tuck into their supper. Right now, however, there was a subject to be broached.

"Oh, Beauteous Creature, I have got you here, apart from for your welcome company, to tell you about what might just be a miracle."

"Suspense, suspense."

"I met today the most extraordinary young man. I truly believe a genius, or at least a genius in the making. You know, I feel I know what it must have been like to meet Mozart, although this young fellow is in no sense vulgar."

"Go on, Douglas, tell me more, stop beating about the bush and get on with it."

"This young chap, called Derick Bilston, a local lad who I met here earlier on this evening, lives in Macclesfield. He has developed a computer search engine of such sophistication and complexity that I was unable to believe that he could have done this entirely on his own."

"Did he do it on his own?"

"Without a doubt. We are in on the ground floor with something which I believe could be a re-run of Chirrup. What do you make of that then?"

"I'm listening hard and trying to take it in. Things like this don't happen in real life, we both know that."

"Well, they did with Chirrup, and my judgement is that they will with Far Horizons. That's what he calls it. I am going to meet him in his office tomorrow morning at nine o'clock. If you like, I'll give you the folder he left me. I have taken a good preliminary look at; if you like what you see, why don't you come too?"

"Yes, I'd like to take a look at his folder, but I take your word for it, I would love to come with you to meet this guy. He must need some funding, are we both good for that do you think? What does he need, half a million to get the thing off the ground? Then a good deal more I guess?"

"I don't know yet, but I imagine that's the scale of it. I think, particularly having done Chirrup together, we both know that speed is all. If it needs more because we can see where it is going, we must be prepared to put a lot more into it. Remember, it is going to need some damned good people straight away. By the way, you and I know where to find a few of them, don't we? What do you think?"

"Sounds good to me, I can't wait to meet him. I agree, we must be prepared to do most if not all of the funding for this, it would be a tragedy to have to get one of those greedy vultures in. You know, the ones who think they know it all and as likely as not fuck it up. They are so bloody impatient, once they are in, all they can think of is their exit route. No Douglas my old friend, this is one that could be just right and ripe for you and me, I'm with you on that. And we know that we would both work our socks off for it."

"That's how I see it. You would have to roll up your sleeves and get it out into the market pretty damned fast, before it got trumped by someone else. That's the big danger, and as you doubtless remember, speed is the answer. And bloody first-class people."

"We ought to be prepared to find about fifteen million to be on the safe side, what do you think?"

"I agree, fifteen should do it. Fifty-fifty?"

"Fifty-fifty. And Derick must have a really significant slug of this too."

"I whole-heartedly agree."

"That's that then".

"Get up you old poof and come and shake my hand. I think we might be off to market."

They met and gave each other a friendly peck, then sat down to put away the now cold pizza.

"One more thing though, Douglas. We will have to get a proper comprehensive systems team together as quickly as we can. We need to put real horsepower behind this Derick fellow if we are to stay ahead of the game. That is an absolute priority I think."

Douglas nodded enthusiastically,

"Damn right we will. We must get onto that straight away. Put out the feelers, now, this very moment."

Douglas got up and rang the bell, whereupon the silent glider took the pizzas away to warm them up. Douglas emptied the last drop of champagne into her glass. Five minutes later the boy was back and they had their rather late supper.

The evening was still young, and Marina didn't feel like going home yet. Their discussion had released a lot of adrenalin and it would have been a dreadful anti-climax to have shut up shop then. Douglas spoke.

"Let's get out the Bourbon and have a bit of music. Relax a bit. Later I would like to show you a couple of paintings that I have just bought at Christie's. They are downstairs, I'll show them to you later."

"How exciting, I'd love to be shown your etchings!"

"Are you in a Mozart mood, or maybe Bach?"

"Since you ask, I would really love to hear the Archduke. For me, Beethoven says it all, and that trio is probably my favourite piece of music. Well, anyway, it is this evening. And a glass of bourbon would be perfection."

They were both pleased and felt fulfilled by an evening in which they didn't have to keep up a chat about nothing but could still enjoy each other's company in vocal silence. Douglas particularly liked the old recording of this work by Wilhelm Kempff, Henryk Szeryng and Pierre Fournier made in nineteen seventy. He called this up as if by magic on his superb audio system, and they both listened with rapt attention.

As silence fell, they went downstairs and Marina was shown in the drawing room, propped up against a leg of Douglas's prized Bösendorfer grand piano, two paintings. One was by Claude Monet of Vétheuil painted in eighteen eighty- eight, the other was by John Anthony Park, of St Ives harbour painted in nineteen thirty-eight. Both were magnificent works. Marina spoke,

"You know, both of these paintings give enormous pleasure, and it is hard to say which gives the most. One must have cost you millions, while the other probably cost low thousands, yet both deliver wonderful joy regardless of their monetary value. I am very drawn to Mr Park's work you know."

"I agree with you, but one must have a Monet, don't you think?"

"Good night Douglas, see you in the morning. Why don't I swing by here at half past eight and we could go together to Stevens's works?"

"Good idea, I'll see you then."

The sound of the dozen French horns faded away as Marina raced across Derbyshire.

Douglas went back to his study and poured himself a top-up of Bourbon and got out a file from his filing cabinet. He wanted to refresh his mind about the people who had worked for Chirrup to see where they lived and what they were up to now. He then got onto the computer to see what sort of office space was available in Macclesfield. Nothing conclusive came out of this, but it served to keep his flame alive well into the night. He hardly slept at all, a feeling of urgency having grown out of the day's proceedings. He finally slept for a few hours, but woke again early, his mind still preoccupied with a sense that time was not on their side and they would have to get on with things without unnecessary delay. He drifted into the subject of funding. Having sold Chirrup for an unheard-of pile of money, both he and Marina should be well able to provide whatever Far Horizons might need. Realistically he felt that he would be good for twenty million himself if push came to shove, and he could think of no reason why Marina shouldn't be in the same position. It would be important to get a proper handle on that before doing anything. You had to be sure that you were in a position to follow your initial stake with an ability and a willingness to put in a great deal more. If it went bust it would cost them a lot, but not half as much as if they backed it and then couldn't find the next stages of funding. That would result in a fire sale and practically nothing for Douglas and Marina, but a bloody fortune for whoever came to the rescue, if it worked. That was a story both had seen many times. And poor Derick would also get nothing. No, if you did it, you had to be able to see it through. There were just as Marina had said, vultures in the trees, and they were proper bastards, you didn't want to mess with them.

Morning dawned and Marina arrived on the dot of half past eight. A quick cup of coffee and away. The silver Porsche pulled up at Stevens's at three minutes to nine o'clock. Douglas pressed the button to put the hood up while the engine rumbled on to provide the power, then he locked the car and they went into the building and up to the reception desk

CHAPTER NINE

Derick had been in his office since eight o'clock. He had spent the time making sure that all the relevant papers were to hand and he knew where to find anything he may need as back-up. The computer was on and he had called up everything that he thought might be important for Douglas to see. He couldn't see from his window when Douglas arrived because his view was at the back and all he could see was the wall of the next building. He had warned Vera at reception that he was expecting an important visitor and now he just waited. It was five to nine. Please no fit of the jitters. Don't be silly, why should that happen? You've met Douglas and you got on fine. Like Mum said, just be yourself. At that moment, exactly nine o'clock, the telephone went in his room. Mr Dominie and Miss Slade-Knox were in reception, should Vera bring them up? Do I go down, or do I let Vera bring them up? More polite if I go down. He told Vera that he was on his way, and he rushed out of the office and down the stairs.

At the bottom step, he set eyes on Douglas and his unknown companion. Douglas was wearing a pale fawn lightweight suit, linen probably, a sky-blue Hermes tie and a pale cream silk shirt. He looked reasonably respectable and business-like, his ponytail up in a tight man-bun. His companion looked terrifyingly professional, even potentially inquisitorial, but supremely elegant. She looked the epitome of the high-maintenance successful girl. And Derick thought she was truly beautiful. The sort of beauty that you couldn't take your eyes off, he had never before seen hair like that, or if he had, he'd failed to register the fact. But this, Oh My God! He pulled himself together with some difficulty, and greeted Douglas, who replied,

"Hi there, Derick. I want you to meet my old colleague Marina. Marina Slade-Knox. We have worked together for some time and pulled off the odd surprise together. This lady is a real smart cookie."

"Hello Derick, I am so glad to meet you, Douglas has told me about your work and I have read the folder you gave him yesterday."

Derick, feeling distinctly ordinary, swallowed and said,

"Hello, I'm very pleased to meet you both, shall we go on up?"

They all sat in Derick's office, around the screen of his computer. Before they came, Derick had asked Jason if he would bring three cups of black coffee in with a bowl of sugar and a little jug of milk, some spoons, all on a tray. And some biscuits if he could find any. Jason had brought these vital items from home that morning; he wasn't going to be caught out. He knocked on the door and brought his burden in and placed it on the table where Derick had told him it would be. Derick spoke.

"I just wanted you to say hello to Jason Stevens who has helped me from time to time. This is Jason."

The visitors nodded and Derick thanked him. Jason smiled and said hello, then left. At this point and without further delay, they got down to the real business. Douglas and Marina took the whole idea in like lightning, and it wasn't long before they had papers everywhere and were inside the workings of Far Horizons like a couple of surgeons doing life-saving operations. Figurative blood and guts lay everywhere, and the air hummed with intelligent questions and well-considered answers. After about three hours, Douglas turned to Marina and said,

"Well? What do you make of it all then?"

Marina stayed silent and leaned back in her chair. She combed her hand loosely through her immaculate blonde hair and then cupped her chin in the palm of the other slender hand.

"I'm not saying anything because basically I am dumbfounded. Derick, thank you, you have explained all this extremely clearly and I think I now understand it as a concept. And thank you for opening it up so we could see its innards."

Douglas said,

"Me too. So, what do you make of it then?"

Marina continued,

"Good start. Very good. Derick I really don't know, like Douglas said, how you did all this on your own. I am full of admiration. I'd definitely like to help, I think this will fly, and as we all know, speed is of the essence. I'm in, I don't know about you Douglas, but I have my hopes. I'm willing to do it."

Douglas replied immediately,

"I'm in too."

The room fell silent.

Derick tapped the escape key and his machine ticked, clicked and chattered to itself.

Douglas looked at Marina, who returned the gaze. He raised his eyebrows inquisitorially, and Marina nodded gracefully.

Douglas spoke.

"I think we all know this has to get a move on. There isn't time to mess about. Derick, we are both willing to come in and support your efforts. You will need first-class assistance in many areas if we are to beat the clock. The team are the most important component of this next to you, and we are confident that we can help you put that together. We know a lot of the best people in the business. You will need a new bigger office and some more powerful computer equipment, and like I have already said, above all lots of the right people. The list is endless, and we are willing to pull our weight to help make this happen. Having sold our company, Chirrup, to Guzzle recently, we are both in a position to put heavy-weight funds behind this effort, and to get going quickly. That is what we would like, with your agreement, to do. And I would like to reassure you at this stage, we insist that you will have a significant carried interest in the whole thing. That means a good slug of shares at no cost. You've already earned that and we both respect it."

Derick was thrown by this. It was exactly what, and more, that he had barely dared to hope for, and here he was with possible salvation at his gates. What do you say when this sort of thing happens. What he said was,

"Are you sure? Do you really think it might go somewhere?"

Marina answered,

"Derick, yes we do, and we are sure that we want to help you and be part of it. The next step must be to put a plan together, and Douglas and I will do that with your detailed input. But we will take it upon ourselves to get that done, and to put immediate money behind it while we work on the plan. We must all control the finances of this and make sure that as it grows it functions efficiently. Don't worry about that, Douglas and I have been here before and we will make that happen."

Douglas pushed his chair back and got up. Marina did the same.

"Derick, Marina, I just happen to have got lunch ready for us all back at the Old Rectory, it is now twenty past twelve and I think we are all exhausted. Let's take a break for once and go back there for a bite of lunch."

Derick was still only five foot seven inches tall, so it wasn't a huge problem for him to squeeze into the back of the Porsche with the hood down. It was, after all, only a mile and a half to Prestbury. As he sat curled up in that severely limited space in the car, he had to pinch himself to believe that this was true. Furthermore, he was directly behind Marina, and he thought she looked absolutely magically wonderful. The strong growth of strawberry blonde hair swished temptingly close to him as he sat there mesmerised, and he just caught the scent of something exotic.

They arrived at the Old Rectory in no time and trooped up to the same study that Derick had first seen yesterday. This time, he promised himself he would take a good look at that picture that he had spotted during his first meeting with Douglas. There it was in all its vibrant colour and movement. He felt sure it must be a Renoir. There was a print of one very similar to it in the Art department at school. How he loved the magic of a good painting.

The small table was set for the three of them and each sat in one of the Chippendale armchairs. On the table was a salad and some cold salmon. To drink there was sparkling Derbyshire mineral water and there were three elegant cut-glass beakers for this. Ice was in a silver bucket. In the middle of the table was a large shallow silver rose bowl filled with white roses.

Derick's feet had still not made their landing on terra firma, and he was amazed by the life that he was now experiencing. Back to Newton Street after this. What a contrast.

Lunch, though excellent and very professionally prepared, was not a long affair. After half an hour Douglas offered to take Derick back to his office, and that was that. Pumpkin time. There would be much to tell Mum and Dad when he got home.

CHAPTER TEN

Derick went up the stairs at Stevens's and into his little office. How wonderful, there was just the hint of Marina's scent still in the air. Though in his late teens, he had never really got to know a girl. Naturally, he'd spoken to them often enough, but they all seemed either messy or tarty and he could never find anything to say to them. He thought that must be because they had nothing interesting to say about anything, so what was the point? He sat there in his chair and let his mind wander. It was still mulling over the paradox of girls. It had been a major shock to the system to meet Marina. Were many girls like that, he wondered, or was she a one-off? By God she was something. She must be old enough to be my mother but wait a minute. Mum is a bit wrinkled and she's got grey hair and just looks like, well, Mum. But this one, oh my God! He pulled himself up short and decided that mooning about like this would get him nowhere. For heaven's sake, however improbable his present position may seem to him, he reflected again on the fact that he had exerted all that effort for as long as he could remember and he had raised the head of steam to get Far Horizons off the ground. Don't go and mess the whole thing up by getting all gooey over this woman. There must be lots like that out there in the big world, don't be in such a bloody hurry. Anyway, she wouldn't look twice at me. Not a midget like me, no way.

Gradually Derick came down to earth. Not with a bump, just a nice three-point landing. He had work to do, so better get on with it. First he had to clear up all the papers and stuff which he had got out for the other two this morning, then he turned his computer on and got back to the task which had been bothering him yesterday.

A knock at the door. Jason came in.

"Well Derick, what was all that about then?"

"Oh, it was just about where we go from here to get Far Horizons off the ground. I think they are going to help do that. They seem to have done a lot together and built up a business and sold it to Guzzle."

69

At that moment Derrek's mobile rang. It was Marina.

"Derick, good to meet you today. Very positive. I just wanted you to know that we have opened an account at Lloyd's in Mac called Far Horizons Special, and Douglas and I have put a quarter of a million each into it. We are all three, you, me and him, signatories, but I'm sure most of what we do will be online. That's half a million which should underpin our first steps in this new adventure. I will take care of the finances so you can get on with what you are so good at without having to worry about the money. See you very soon."

And she was gone.

"How much did they get for that?"

"I've no idea, but it must have been a good bit I should think. They didn't tell me and I thought I had better not ask. I will find out one day if all this does go ahead, but I am finding it hard to get my head around this."

"Where did you all go off to for lunch?"

"We went to his house in Prestbury. I went in the back of his 911 and she sat in front with him."

"A bit of a looker, I thought, didn't you?"

"I don't know, probably, yeah."

"Come on! You don't see things like that in Mac, I can tell you. Tell me, when did you last see a thing like that?"

"Yeah, you're probably right."

"What was that Porsche like then? Fast was it?"

"We only went a mile or so. I don't know, but there's not much room in it, I can tell you that."

Jason left, mystified. He muttered to himself about what the hell was going on. His dad Cecil Stevens had no idea what it was and nor had Stan. Derick hadn't said too much to Cecil, and anyway, his dad would probably stay quiet about it.

Meanwhile, immediately after lunch, Douglas and Marina settled down to go through records in Douglas's study. They looked out some of the early stuff from the beginnings of Chirrup to refresh their minds on the details. Douglas was also hunting for records of staff and making lists of people he knew or was aware of, who would be vital for the building up of Far Horizons. Between them, by six o'clock they had some basic fundamentals sketched out and were starting to divide up some of the most urgent tasks between them. When they had earlier opened the bank account at Lloyd's in the name of Far Horizons Special, they had felt it important to include Derick as a signatory. Cheques would require any two to sign, but most payments would doubtless be made online and Marina had volunteered herself to be Miss Money-Bags. The two of them went fifty-fifty on putting the immediate half a million into that account. Neither thought that would do much beyond turning the light switches on, but it was an immediate gesture and that was its true purpose. Immediately after lunch Douglas had been in touch with Hallam's the Estate Agents just to get an up-to-date idea of the cost of good modern Office property in the area. They had promised to come back with a representative range of ideas.

By the end of that day, the ship was getting under way.

Derick returned home at about half past six, his head still in a spin, a mixture made up of equal parts of apprehension and optimism, with optimism in the ascendant. He went into the house and was immediately aware of the smell of lamb chops. His lunch had been pretty insubstantial, so he was ready for a bit of Mum's home cooking. He went into the kitchen and planted a kiss on his mother's cheek.

"Oh, that is nice. Thank you my darling. Come here, I want to give you a hug."

"Where's Dad?"

"He's upstairs having a shower. He'll be down in a minute."

"I think we are going to have to get a couple of beers out and give you a sherry. There's a bit to talk about when Dad comes down, or if you have to be in here in the kitchen, it can wait until we have our tea."

"Ooh, that sounds exciting, I can't wait."

The sound of heavy shoes on the slender stairway announced Stan's arrival.

"Hello, son, all going well, I hope?"

"If Mum can come in, I think we all need a drink and then we must sit down. I have got something to tell you."

Stan went in search of the sherry and the beers, after all, he knew the ropes and was in charge of this rare occurrence. It was a rarity any time, particularly mid-week, so there must be something special that the boy wants to tell us. I can tell him that

Mr Brandridge has confirmed what he said about the ugly Chinese pot, so we've both got news. I wonder what his is. They all sat around the table which Ethel had pulled out ready for their tea. They sat down and looked at each other. Stan said,

"I'll start the ball rolling. Mr Brandridge has told me that he believes his valuation is correct for that ugly old pot. So that's good news. Derick, we should be able to do something for you."

"Well done Dad. Now, I have got a bit of news for you two as well. You know the guy who I went to see yesterday? As you know Dad, he came back this morning with a woman who he has worked with before. They made a mountain of money together, it seems. They sold their business called Chirrup to Guzzle for a huge sum, I have no idea yet how much, but it must have been hundreds of millions I think."

"I can't understand how anybody can do that. It is quite beyond me and it makes no sense at all to me. I am used to doing a good day's work and getting a pay packet at the end of the week. A good one too, but this I just do not understand. I really don't. But, never mind, go on son."

"Well, the thing is they came over to my room at Stevens's this morning and fairly romped through my work. They are really clever and they understood everything. I was amazed, because I know how tricky the whole thing is, but they went through it like a dose of salts. And they liked it. We all went back in his Porsche to his enormous place at Prestbury for lunch, and they rang later to say they've already done it."

"Done what, son?"

"They've done it, they've opened a new bank account for Far Horizons at Lloyds in Mac, and put half a million in it."

Stan put his glass on the table and stood up. He walked back and forth across the room, then sat down again.

"Did I hear you right? Put half a million in the bank for you?"

"Yes, you did, but it's not for me, it's for my project, but to get it out I am also authorised, so it is all OK. The first thing we are going to do is beef up the technical team, systems blokes to stiffen up my development activity. Lots of them. We will really have to go at it fast to stay ahead, and that will be the first thing we do. We'll find new temporary accommodation for them and me before we get settled somewhere finally."

"Son, I just don't know what to say. If you've got it right that's wonderful. I am so pleased for you, well done. I would never have thought such a thing could happen, but you tell me it has."

"It has."

The chops were a bit burnt, and the greens were a bit soggy, but their tea was the happiest meal any of them could remember. Stan went and got more drinks and they bubbled their way through till it was time to get up and see what might be on the telly. Derick spoke again,

"You really ought to sell that pot you know, you could pay off the mortgage and you could find another house for the next part of your life. I shall find somewhere to lodge so will be out of your hair, but somewhere very close. You can look forward to a new life if you pop that old pot. Go on, do it. You're always saying it's an ugly old thing, and a couple of hundred thousand smackers would be a Godsend wouldn't it?"

Stan pondered this.

"Yes, I think you are right. We can put something else in my little corner I made for it. Something nice this time I think. Tell me Derick, do you think the new company will pay you now that it has got some money?"

"I am sure it will, but we haven't talked about that yet. It has all happened so quickly, there are a lot of things to discuss, and that is one of them. I shall have to learn to drive too, because I'm sure I will have to travel a bit. I'll have to get some smarter clothes too, but that can all wait while we see how this goes."

Stan thought about this and reckoned that Derick was right. If they were doing this to back his idea they would hardly treat him other than well, and by all accounts they seemed decent and honest people. Well, you can't really tell, but that is what I feel. He said,

"Cecil Stevens says Jason said the girl was a real looker, is she?"

"I don't know, he's probably right."

Derick saw in his mind the most beautiful creature he had ever set eyes on.

"I couldn't really say, is that what Jason said?"

"Yes, she fair knocked him out. You'll be moving into a new office then, will you? You'll probably very soon have a good few people working with you, and all sorts. That'll need more space, and somewhere a bit smarter and more modern I should think."

Derick's mobile rang. It was Marina again.

"That's them. I must go upstairs."

He ran up the precarious stairs and into his room and slammed the door as he answered the call.

"Hello."

"Derick, things are moving, I want you to come with me to San Francisco the day after tomorrow. There are some people you and I ought to take a look at. I'll meet you at Newton Street at eight o'clock in the morning and we'll drive to Heathrow together. I'll brief you on the journey. Have you got a passport?"

Thank God he had. Thanks to a school trip to New York on a reciprocal with another school there, so not only did he have a passport, he had a visa as well.

"Yes, I do, and an American visa, see you then eight o'clock. How smart do I have to be?"

"Not smart, just clean. I'll meet you at lunch time tomorrow at Stevens's and we'll sort you out. It has to be done I'm afraid, nothing personal. Bye."

CHAPTER ELEVEN

In the wee small hours, there was a lot of fantasising going on at Newton Street. Off to San Francisco by God. Well I don't know. I do know one thing, when we have got both the passports I will be able to see how old she is. I am nearly nineteen, I guess her to be about thirty, maybe twenty-nine. I don't know, but that is only eleven or ten years more than me. Dad's thirteen years older than Mum for Heaven's sake. But that is the other way around isn't it? So? Derick was finding it awfully difficult to clear his mind and get back to normal, but he knew he had to do that, there were no other options. Or were there? No there bloody well weren't.

At half past twelve the next day, Vera rang up to Derick's room to say that Miss Slade-Knox was in reception. Derick nearly burst a blood vessel with excitement, then managed to calm himself down. Be cool, don't make an ass of yourself, she would be very quick to pick that up. For God's sake be cool and collected, go down slowly and just be yourself, like Mum always says. He rounded the corner at the bottom of the stairs, and there before him was Marina. She was dressed in a slim calf-length sage green skirt and a silk shirt with a linen coat on top. There was only the Tiffany cross and the Vacheron, no jewellery beyond that and a small pair of diamond stud earrings. She was, as always, a picture. Derick cleared his throat and prepared to greet her in the most normal way he could muster.

"Hello Marina, I'm ready when you are. Thanks for this."

The necessary shopping was done at lightning speed and with precision. Marina knew exactly what to get and the whole thing was done in an hour and a half. Derick felt pleased. Oddly he didn't feel out of place wearing Marina's idea of what the Lad around Silicon Valley might be expected to wear.

All done and dusted. Back to the office. Heathrow tomorrow.

Marina and Derick flew out together to San Francisco in business class. The journey was for Derick a completely new experience, given the luxury of Business. For Marina it was a tiresome routine. Had she been alone she would have gone First, but out of kindness to Derick, she elected for the lower grade, in order not to overwhelm him. What did it matter, they were both of normal size, so there was plenty of room? And the Lanson was the same. Derick had now grown taller and was five foot seven and a half inches. Not tall, but a whole lot better than before. He noticed that Marina generally wore flat heels, so they were now on level terms. That felt good. And to have her by his side felt even better. Now that a dark beard had grown on his face, which he shaved every day religiously, he looked more than his years. This was a considerable relief. It was from now on extremely unlikely that he would again be mistaken for her son. It had happened once at the beginning, and each had been annoyed by it, for different reasons, but both to do with age. While at Heathrow she had handed him the passports to look after when she went to powder her hair and brush her nose. She did this because she thought they might be called, and passports might be needed for some reason or other. Derick took a good look as soon as she was out of sight. Just as he thought, she was eight years his senior. That's nothing, he thought, and was considerably encouraged by this discovery.

When they arrived at San Francisco International SFO, they went straight to their hotel and took the rest of the day and evening off. Marina briefed Derick thoroughly about the people they had gone there to meet, and he felt at least well informed and up to the task. She reminded him gently that he was the star in this exercise, so there would be no need to be anything other than himself. She said,

"These people will respect you, so you don't have to make an effort to impress them, I have already done that."

For Derick this was a dream. He remembered the time he had gone to New York on the school trip with a dozen other boys from Macclesfield. They had stayed in a large impersonal block in Queen's, two boys to a room, very rough and ready and tiny hard beds. They had spent the days being driven around in a mini-bus from place to place, all to a time schedule, and to fit in with meals in pizza bars and by hot-dog stands. They had gone to Central Park and walked for a quarter of an hour, seen nothing but a few people from offices jogging around with headsets between stints in their offices, dressed for the occasion. They had taken a brief trip around the Park in horse drawn landaus pulled by down at heel tired old horses. They had been to Times Square and tried to read the billboards that told what shows were on. It had been difficult to see out of the windows if you weren't on the outside. Derick had been on the aisle side and had therefore seen almost nothing. They had gone to the Bronx to see the home of the New York Yankees. They also visited the New York Jets and the New York Giants. None of this meant a thing to Derick who quickly became bored with the whole business. He was glad to get back to Macclesfield and his mother's cooking and away from the dirty streets of New York, with the steam coming out of grilles and manhole covers everywhere. And the towering overpowering skyscrapers all around you. He didn't like the place at all, and everybody seemed to be in such a hurry and to be so unfriendly. A tiny high spot was when they went and stood in the entrance porch of Tiffany's and listened to a young beautiful and intense looking girl violinist playing Bach sonatas, a student from the Juilliard school earning the wherewithal to continue her training. This was the only human personal thing that Derick remembered from a short period of absolute chaos and turbulence. New York, he had not enjoyed. But this, the tip top of what San Francisco had to offer was something else. What an adventure.

Lying on his back in his ocean-going super-comfortable bed in his ultra-luxurious room, with his hands between his head and the pillows, gazing up at the ceiling, Derick thought the contrast is truly amazing. I have never in my whole life been in a room like this or slept in a bed like this. A man could get used to it.

After a refreshing shower the next morning, he got dressed and came downstairs. Marina was already at a table and she beckoned him over. The breakfast was wonderfully un-English. There were all sorts of pots with creamy or fruity substances in them accompanied by wordy write-ups on their sides telling of the wonders which would occur if you ate their product. Slices of cheese, pastries, all sorts of things which Derick had never seen before at breakfast time were there on a large island in the middle of the room, around which were a number of slim and fit people picking the least fattening of the myriad offerings before them. It was to Derick slightly bizarre. What was wrong with a good old English breakfast?

CHAPTER TWELVE

The few days they spent in the Valley went well. They had cut ice, and both felt up-beat. At least two of those that they had met seemed interested and well capable of doing what would be required of them. In both cases there had been no problem about re-locating to England. Such individuals were used to going where fate demanded in a fluid and well-paid environment. There would doubtless be other trips to other places to pick up the entire team, but this trip had, it seemed, taken the immediate urgency out of the equation.

They landed back at Heathrow and both felt to some degree jet lagged. A day at home would soon put that right. Marina took melatonin, which she swore by. Derick thought that nothing on God's Earth would put this girl out. Miss Roller Coaster.

When they re-surfaced the next day, Douglas called and summoned them both to the Old Rectory that evening. He asked Marina to collect Derick so that they could have a get together at six o'clock, to which she agreed, and at the appointed hour the three of them sat down in the now familiar study at the Old Rectory. Douglas opened up.

"Could we start with a very quick de-brief on your trip. I gather from what you've already told me that it went well. Well done you two, I knew it would."

Derick and Marina both gave a short dissertation on their trip, and then they left the floor to Douglas who had made it plain that he had something entirely different that he wanted to bounce off them.

"Thanks for that, it's gone well, I think. I have a completely different subject I want to raise with the two of you. It is connected, but it is much more than that."

Douglas was a nosy being. He made it his business to know exactly what was going on in all sorts of places, trivial and important. He spoke.

"I was talking the other day, while you were over there, to Mr Dewthorpe at the Derbyshire County Council. He looks after property and probably does some other things too. He is a simple soul and I would guess honest, and I imagine he doesn't say anything unless he is sure of his ground. He's a Councillor too and I think an Independent, but I'm not sure, anyway, that's not important."

Douglas stopped and sauntered over to a drinks tray which his man had put there.

"Glass of something?"

Two voices said they could kill a beer. Douglas turned the bottle-top off and gave them both one of his fine tumblers and the opened bottles of Drunk Skunk. He took a Bourbon for himself, with a splash of water.

"Now, to the point. This Mr Dewthorpe told me that as always they are short of money, and he had had an idea which he was sure the Council were prepared to back."

Douglas took a sip and rolled it around his mouth while he thought.

"Look, this may sound irrelevant and a bit too big, but here goes. You know that great big ruin all boarded up, called Old Dale Park?"

Melina and Derick looked at each other and nodded. Douglas went on.

"Well, they are willing to sell the whole thing, but they think it may be too far gone to interest anybody. Actually, Dewthorpe thought he was picking my brains to try to help him find a buyer. My immediate thought was to do it ourselves."

"Isn't that a bit rich?"

"I don't know yet, but I think it is worth taking a good look at it."

"What do you propose to do with it, Douglas, It's a huge place and would need to be totally re-done. What the Hell might that cost I wonder?"

Marina sounded sceptical, but not entirely closed on the subject. Douglas continued.

"My idea is that it would make a wonderful location for a hi-tech colony, a sort of Silicon Valley of the Peak District. There's more to it than that. You know the government scheme to make Charter Cities, or Enclaves, Locations, whatever they might call them. I mean places which concentrate the best of industry and set their own rules on such things as tax and corporate affairs. I think this place could be one of those, and we could straight away house Far Horizons in one of the buildings on the estate which is habitable and up and running. I believe the caretakers' house would do. Eventually we would fill the rest of the place with the crème de la crème of hi-tech front-runners. What do you make of that?"

"Wow, that's a surprise, and I think it sounds interesting. What do we do? Is it worth us all meeting this Mr Dewthorpe, or has he done all he can. Who's the big cheese?"

"I don't know yet, but I'll soon find out. I think it would pay to keep our powder dry for a bit. We wouldn't want to give anything away until we were ready to go, would we?"

Derick had listened spellbound and said very little. This was not his field, but it sounded as though it should be a goer. He definitely liked what he had heard and was glad to be part of it. But would he be? How could he be, he had no money? Douglas spoke again,

"Derick, you have got to be an equal part of this, the whole thing sprang out of your idea, don't worry, we'll see you all right. By the way, are you two OK for time? I could go on a bit if you like and tell you what he let slip."

Marina said,

"Please do, I am being killed by the suspense."

"Well, after our more formal discussion, which he had asked for by the way, he relaxed a bit and gave me a bit of the background to this. Apparently, it is called Old Dale Park because a chancer called Dale bought it in about eighteen forty something. He had made a serious fortune in cotton and wanted to leave his mark, so he bought the place, much as it looks now, and rebuilt it from top to toe leaving the eighteenth century exterior unaltered. He did everything up to a very high standard on the inside though, and he changed its name to Dale Park. Now, because of cotton and the way things were then, his memory is tarred with slavery in America and low wages which were almost as bad as slavery, in India. His statue in Buxton and another in Mac were torn down a few years ago, and the Council are embarrassed by all this. They now just want out. You may have noticed that the Dale Building in Mac is now the Ungwalawa Building and various Dale Crescents and Roads have been renamed. One is even called Blair Street now. He told me a bit about the history of Dale Park."

Derick and Marina were by now intrigued to know more.

"Go on, you can't stop now. Tell all."

"It seems that it was built originally in about seventeen fifty, by an old India hand who was high up in the East India Company, and made a massive fortune from all that. The site was a village called Pemstone, and this man a Mr Burk who changed his name to de Burgh when he got a baronetcy, did what was called emparkment. He flattened the village and built another in the same style as the house, a couple of miles away in the hollow to the north of the present house. That's the village that is there now and what a good job he made of it too. Then he had the Park designed and made by Capability Brown in as I say, about seventeen fifty. The beautiful lake dates from his time, but apart from the layout of the Park, nothing else remains of his work. Our friend was clearly not short of money, because he had Robert Adam do the house. I gather much of his work is still discernible but in poor condition. I am told that it could be saved partly, and the rest could be copied."

"What a story. Does it go on?"

"Are you all right still for time?"

"I'm not letting you stop. Go on."

"As can happen, this guy had no family, so it passed to cousins, also de Burgh, and they had no children, so it eventually went to another cousin called d'Arcy. Yes, apparently that was his real name. He had no children either, so his widow sold it to the Dales, and that is where we came in. The Dales, who were the cause of the present day hoo-ha about the statues and all the street and buildings' names, changed its name to Dale Park, it had been called Pemberley up until then."

"And after that?"

"Dale's only son Augustus was killed in the charge of the Light Brigade at Balaclava as a cornet in the Seventeenth Lancers, one of the dozen or so Old Etonians to fall in that disaster. So, yet again there was no heir, and Mrs Dale just wanted to get out. It went downhill very quickly. At some point it had been used as an isolation hospital, and then in the Boer War and again in the First War it was a Military Hospital. After that, it was a Boys' Prep School which went bust, then a hotel just at the time of the Market Crash in nineteen twenty-nine, which also went bust almost immediately. It had very little value then, and the Pitt-Curnows bought it. He was Sir George Pitt and he married an American cousin of the Rockefeller family called Frederika Curnow, and they took on the name Pitt-Curnow. Apparently great-grandfather Havilland Curnow was a miner from Cornwall and he took the name of Curnow meaning Cornwall, at Ellis Island, then did a bit of mining before joining his cousin in Standard Oil. George died before the war and the son, who picked up a knighthood on the way, Sir Ralph and his wife Lady Sylvia had it until he died and she moved out. It went downhill again in a very undignified way, and that brings us to now."

"Well, thanks for the history lesson. I think it is definitely worth following up. I wonder if the government is really thinking as you say, or do you think they might just be talking about it? Hauling up a flag to see who salutes it."

"That's one of the things we shall have to get clear about. I've e-mailed the MP, Gerald Grantham, to get his view on this. He's a bit of an old buffer, but he ought to be able to find out. I'll keep at him until I get an answer, then I'll see who else I need to talk to."

The meeting finally broke up and all were excited about Far Horizons and about Old Dale Park. There was a lot to think about.

Douglas's parting shot was,

"I think I'll do a little beavering. I wonder if there is a vital bit of real estate near the Park which I could buy that might scupper their chances of doing a deal with someone else? A field, a private road, something to stuff old Dewthorpe! We could do with a bit of leverage here."

Derick was dropped back at Newton Street by Marina, and he went into the sitting room and sat silent. His mother and father were in the kitchen. She spoke,

"Where have you been? We were worried about you."

"I've been with Douglas and Marina. Another idea has come up. I would have thought it was a bit far-fetched until I met those two. Now it sounds OK."

Derick explained the idea for buying Old Dale Park. His father said,

"I just don't know. This is a totally different world that you have got yourself into. I can't understand it at all, I really can't. It doesn't sound like what I call work at all, it's more like fantasy land, but don't let me put you off. Who knows, these two might just be the answer to a prayer. Or a curse. It's hard to know which, from where I stand."

"Well, Dad, I intend to go along with it, remember, I've been out to Silicon Valley with Marina, and she is very impressive, and she knows everybody. I mean everybody, from the governor to the sweeper. And they all love her too. That girl is a phenomenal piece of work, I tell you."

"Like Mum said, you should know. And what about the queer one?"

"He's full of ideas and doesn't waste a minute. As soon as an idea appears, he's off like a mad thing. Except he isn't a mad thing, he's as clever as they come too. I intend to go along with them and throw my lot into it all. Well, I have already. We are getting things moving at a staggering rate."

CHAPTER THIRTEEN

Mr Dewthorpe sat in his office in County Hall, overlooking parkland by Smedley Street in the centre of Matlock. He sat and mulled over the meeting he had had with Mr Dominie. He thought to himself about that dead albatross around his neck, Old Dale Park. A strange cove that Mr Dominie, a poof of course, but we mustn't say that now. He seemed to know what he was talking about. It's hard to tell with Americans, was he serious or was he just passing the time of day? I certainly thought, because I was tipped off, that he was genuine. I wouldn't have got in touch with him unless I thought it made some kind of sense. When you're desperate, desperate measures. But as I say, you can never be sure. I think if he can, he will help. He may know someone in America, or even here who might bite, but it is a long shot. Who would want the place? Far too big and nearly falling down too. Not much use as a hotel, besides, it tried that a long time ago and got nowhere. Much too complicated and falling apart for that. The maintenance must be colossal. Flats Maybe? It would make hundreds of them, but who would want to move into one up here? Particularly if it was as expensive as it would have to be? No, I just can't see anybody wanting that. I think we are stuck with it. Knock it down? Seems a pity, but it really isn't much use to anyone. Anyway, it is Grade One listed, so that puts the kibosh on pretty well everything. Looking back, it was a great mistake to sell off the stable block, but we needed the money and that seemed like a good way to raise quite a decent bit. But now that we want to sell the whole thing, that bit right in the middle that we don't own makes it even harder. Who's going to tolerate something like a leisure centre or some bloody pop music place right on their doorstep? No one in his right mind would touch it, it would take what little value there might be in the place right down to bloody nothing. You don't take a thing like that on to have bloody noise and stuff, drugs maybe, heavy boozing, loud dreadful pop music and lots of young trash all over the place peeing up against your walls and fucking in the flower beds. The whole thing is a lost cause and a nightmare. At least at the moment there isn't anything too awful going on at the stables, but it would be a time bomb if you went and bought the place. Maybe we should try to buy the stable block back before getting the whole thing on the market. We don't even know who owns it now or what their plans might be. It would be just as harmful if it's derelict, to us, as it would be with screaming demented youth. I'll bring that up at the next Council Meeting, but there's also the problem of where's the bloody money coming from? Damn, I've missed this month's meeting, it will have to wait until next month. If I can get it on the agenda. Everyone is so bored with this whole Dale Park thing, I think most of them would rather forget it and talk about something else. What is it to them? Out of sight out of mind. I've been properly lumbered.

Douglas got in the 911 and drove off to Old Dale Park. He thought it was time to go and have another proper mosey around. See just what was there and try to discover if there were any obvious weak points where he could get the better of the Council. He wasn't aware of anything, but until you had a good look and poked your nose in, talked to a few people, you didn't really know. He parked the Porsche and started to walk all around the place, missing nothing. At the end of a couple of hours he was frustrated and disappointed. There was no evidence that he could see of anything that might give him a bit of leverage. Gerald Grantham's office had come back and suggested a meeting in his constituency office in West Bank Road Macclesfield at the weekend, how would four o'clock on Saturday afternoon suit them? Grantham hadn't given any opinion on the question of Charter Cities, but if there was nothing in it, why have a meeting? Douglas confirmed the appointment. Meanwhile he got in touch with a couple of local Estate Agents to see if there was any low down on Old Dale Park. So far he had drawn a blank, but perseverance was his second name and his nature. He rang Derick and asked him if he would like to join him at the meeting with the MP. If anything interesting were to come out of it in connection with Far Horizons, it would be better if Derick heard it from the horse's mouth. Derick jumped at the chance. Having considered what Douglas had said about making a Charter property out of Old Dale Park, Derick was keen to follow it up and he hoped something might come of it. Even to him, it appeared to make a great deal of sense and offer perhaps a unique opportunity. Douglas also asked Marina to come and she accepted without hesitation. Better get on with it and see whether it flies or doesn't. Good start. She agreed to pick Derick up in her car as she went through to the meeting.

After a hectic week, Derick welcomed the arrival of Saturday and a whole weekend; he looked forward to meeting Gerald Grantham. This would be an entirely new experience, among many new experiences of the recent weeks. He had never even known the name of his local MP before now, and none of his family had either met or even thought about that man or that role. Stan and Ethel had been tribal Labour supporters all their lives, following in their families' footsteps. This they had done without any serious thought. It was just, to them, the way life was. Derick thought that a bicycle ride in the morning over to Old Dale Park might be worthwhile. Not for any particularly good reason, mainly because he had the time and was still very curious about the place. No harm in having a poke around.

He rode over to the house with a sense of curiosity and enthusiasm. As it hove into sight, he said to himself, me in that place? Come on, pigs will fly sooner than that. But he knew that there was an outside chance of such a strange happening, so spurred himself on to take another look. Having put his bike on the grass by the great pillared entrance, he started to walk all around the vast plot. There were buildings everywhere around the back, and there was also the caretakers' house standing on its own, out of the way, which looked cared for and possibly lived in; there was a tired looking nondescript car parked across the end, and an abandoned wheelbarrow next to it. That was where they would start off with Far Horizons if it all came to anything. Close to the main house at the back was the very elegant and symmetrical stable block and coach houses standing on the neatly cobbled yard surrounding it. He noticed that it had a low chain at about knee height surrounding it and that its high doors had at some time been painted a different colour from that which remained on bits of the house. It was shabby, but just looked different. The doors were all shut and looked as though they hadn't been opened for a very long time. There was no sign of life anywhere. He wandered over to get a closer look, and spotted a notice nailed to the main entrance of the grooms' quarters in the centre. It said simply, in black paint on a piece of bare chipboard about two feet square, Private Keep Out. It was crooked and falling apart. After an hour of snooping, he left and returned home for his dinner of chicken thighs and baked potato. He thought to himself that if he ate any more of those, he would fly.

Marina picked Derick up at half past three, intending to be at the Conservative constituency office in plenty of time so that she and Douglas and Derick could compare notes before going in, and hatch a plan should they judge that to be necessary.

The Porsche was already there and Douglas was in it reading some papers. When he saw the Bentley he got out and greeted the two of them warmly.

"Good that we've got a few minutes, I got this from the Estate Agents. I now know a bit more about this place. It seems that a mystery man owns the stables, right in the middle. I am trying to find a way of getting to him without raising suspicions. It would be wonderful if we could buy that on the QT. That'd fix them."

Derick chimed in.

"Well. I was up there this morning and the whole place seems dead. I think someone lives in the caretakers' house, and the stable and coach house block looks all closed up and a bit derelict. It's painted a different colour and it has a scruffy notice nailed on the door saying Private Keep Out, so not much goes on there, whoever owns it."

"Well done you. I'll find out who it is that owns it and we'll have a go at him."

They went in and were shown into Gerald Grantham's room. He was a portly well-fed gentleman in his sixties, on the last lap before the delivery of his knighthood and well-heeled retirement. He wore a mossy tweed suit and a tie that had seen better days. On the desk were a very few papers and a photograph of Mrs Grantham who looked every bit the country MP's wife. Smart casual, nothing too grand. A good mixer and a reliable conversationalist. Well-practised and good at speaking to 'them'. Slightly ridiculed by 'us'. On the walls of the comfortable little room were signed photographs of Winston Churchill, Mrs

Thatcher, and Boris. In the middle of the long wall was a print of the Simon Elwes portrait of Her Majesty Queen Elizabeth the Second. It too had been signed, but only by the artist beside the printed signature of the Monarch.

The three visitors were keen to get down to business, but the MP showed little inclination to oblige. They began to doubt whether he knew anything at all about Charter Cities. However, after an indecently long interval of warm air, he started to address the question before them.

"I am interested in your concept of using Old Dale as one of the proposed Charter establishments. It is no use to anybody as it is and is an embarrassment to the County Council. It is a bit small for an independent self-governing business establishment, but on the other hand it may well serve the purpose of proving the Charter concept. If it succeeds, as I think it would, the case would be made, and the scheme could be rolled out on a much larger scale. I think there is mileage in this, and I will have a talk with the Minister and with the PM and come back to you. I think the ambition to do this was covered rather obliquely in the Gracious Speech. It is an idea that has some legs as far as I can see."

Recovering from the astonishment that Grantham knew a bit about it, Douglas reaffirmed the reason why they were interested, just to make sure the old man's memory didn't fail later.

"As you know, our plan is to turn it into a hi-tech Charter City with Far Horizons as the opening inhabitant. Time is of the essence, as is secrecy at this stage. I should add that we three are the sole owners of Far Horizons and we shall also be the sole owners of Old Dale if we can pull this off. At some stage we shall open it up for outside investment, but not until the case is demonstrably made."

They left with a spring in their steps.

"So far so good, I think."

Derick added,

"He surprised me, I thought it went very well once he got going."

Marina said,

"Yes, we can't complain, I just hope he has a bit of clout and actually does something. Hop in Derick, home."

As he toyed with his supermarket hamburger at teatime, Derick said,

"Mum and Dad, I got the impression that we got somewhere this afternoon. I have no idea how much this old boy counts at Westminster, but it felt like a good start to me. At first it was terribly slow, we all thought he knew nothing about it and was just going to talk us out of the meeting. But he made good sense in the end, so we've all got our fingers crossed."

Stan said,

"This is all beyond me, a bit like a film. So you actually had a meeting with our Tory MP. Well I never, what would your grandfather have said if he knew that? He said they were all bastards. Polite and friendly, but bastards all the same. When your back was turned."

"Dad, it's not that simple. I think he'll be as good as his word, though we can have no idea of whether it will fly or not."

Derick's mobile rang. It was Douglas.

"Derick, listen. I've found out who owns the stable and coach house block. It's a guy called Ernie Shelton. He has a gambling business and advertises on the local telly. It's called Katch As Kan. He also has a great barn of a place on the outskirts of Matlock which is a sort of teenage rave club, huge and noisy and he has had trouble with the locals wanting to shut it down. I have found out that he is at the moment going through a really nasty divorce, I was told he had been caught at it by his wife. It may have been the other way around, I can't quite honestly remember, but no matter. So, the iron may be hot, time to strike."

"That didn't take long! Well done, it looks as though there may be a chance here. Like Far Horizons, the timing is going to be important, we must get in there before the County Council wake up."

"This guy lives in Matlock, I haven't got his address yet, but I know that I'll have it soon. I think the only thing is to go and see him as soon as I know where he is. That's what I'll do. I think his plan with the stable block must have been to do another teenage club, but he must have been shot down by the Council on that one. We shall see. With a divorce going on, he's going to need a bit of money too."

Derick sat back and reflected. This is a runaway train.

CHAPTER FOURTEEN

Ethan Samuels and Dan Abramski were in a champagne bar in Silicon Valley. They had both just been contacted by Marina Slade-Knox and given each other's phone numbers. She wanted them both to join this English company Far Horizons in a place called Macclesfield in Derbyshire. Would they please talk between themselves and come back to her with any questions and a preliminary conclusion. They had been told that the new company was already up and running and had some initial revenue. It had also now established a powerful team of systems and technical people who had proved their worth in household names. They were now in place at Macclesfield and the project was flying.

As they understood it, the company created algorithms which search out compatibilities between markets and production facilities in a wide range of countries with differing systems, all over the world. A very powerful search engine which takes the heavy lifting out of analysis and the hunt for suitable markets, product by product. She had said that they were at the stage where they needed to get out into the world fast to be sure of stealing a march on any other outfit that was going down the same hole. She had also said that funding was in place and that she and Douglas had been the engines behind Chirrup which they had sold to Guzzle. Ethan and Dan remembered that case with unabashed admiration. They were both inclined to imagine that Far Horizons could go the same way, with the two of them at the centre of it. That was certainly appealing. Just where was this Macclesfield then? The more they thought about it, the more they realised that there would be other applications for this company, and the key was to stiffen the team with the right people fast and get on with it. They both agreed to sleep on it and reconvene as soon as they had got their heads fully around it and, in particular, worked out for themselves what the scope was for widening and deepening the Far Horizons' offering. They parted with optimism and incipient excitement.

Meanwhile, Douglas was sitting in Ernie Shelton's office, in a dark maroon button-backed leather wing chair of unhappily gross proportions. Ernie sat behind an over-sized over-ornate dark wood matching maroon leather-topped desk, in rolled-up shirtsleeves with an open neck over which a tuft of chest hair protruded in a slightly comical manner. An extensive equestrian tattoo adorned each hairy brown arm. He was a large man with an open ingratiating smile on a larger than life podgy face. His welcome was effusive and formulaic. Douglas surprisingly up until this moment remained relatively silent, other than to offer brief greetings. The room was dark apart from the desktop which had a gold coloured table light on one side, shining over a neat pile of papers in front of Ernie. A cut glass chandelier hung in the centre of the plaster work on the ceiling, but was not switched on.

Douglas explained briefly what the purpose was of his visit, expanding but a little on what he had already told Ernie on the telephone when he had set up the meeting.

"So, you want to buy my stable block up at Dale then, do you?"

Ernie opened the batting, hoping to find out why Douglas was interested in that property and how strong his interest was. Douglas answered,

"Ernie, if I may call you that, I want to preserve the best part of that whole place and to do it I could move a small business I have up there. The rest of it isn't any use to anyone and it wouldn't surprise me if in the end they knocked it all down. That's it really, there isn't much more to say, only that of course I like the place and admire the architecture and would like to keep it going for the future."

"That's much why I bought it. It hasn't been the best of investments, I have to agree, but it is unique. Where else do you find such a perfect property of a size that is manageable?"

"I think we agree there. How about my buying it from you then? I could act quite quickly if that was any help to you."

"The trouble is Douglas, I don't really want to sell it. How would a short lease do?"

"That's a tough one Ernie. I don't think I could justify spending money making it work for my purposes unless I had a freehold. It wouldn't make sense from my point of view."

"There's always a long lease, and I wouldn't mind committing to a buy-back so you wouldn't be stuck with it."

Douglas scented progress. Best just keep him talking and he'll talk himself into a sale. Silence reigned for a bit, then Douglas spoke.

"I could of course just leave my business where it is, it works perfectly well there. I simply thought Dale could be a good idea and it occurred to me that the idea could help you too. You know, word gets around."

"Oh I don't know about that. I'm a rich man Douglas, I don't need anything, but I can see the sense in your wanting to get it. It would make a good office, that's for sure."

"Well then, what about it. A freehold I mean?"

The ball rolled inconclusively and gently back and forth between them, each stage Douglas thought getting closer to a deal, but his judgement said that today would not produce a result. Better leave now and let it cook a bit.

"Well, thanks Ernie, that has been very helpful, but I am sure you can see why only a freehold would work for my purposes. I do entreat you to think about it, I hope you understand that I am serious and would get on with it without hassle and delay or anything like that. I'll leave you in peace now, but you know where I am if you want to talk some more."

With that Douglas left. He couldn't help noticing the pottery horses dotted around the place, and the chamfered glass in the windows with frosted horses decorating some of them. Ernie was obviously a traveller who'd made it big time. He felt that Ernie probably loved doing deals and lived by that. A few days should see him coming back with an agreement to sell; Douglas got the impression that Ernie had lost interest in the stable block. He wondered if his oblique reference to the troublesome divorce had registered, it would have been too impolite to be any more direct than he had been, but it was an important bit of information. Douglas left convinced that Ernie would be back in a day or two. He also noted that Ernie had let slip the name of his estate agent who advised him in his property dealings. Douglas made a mental note to be in touch with this Mr Worrell-Smith so that he could drop the information into his ear that he would be a buyer for the stables. He would let the agent know that he now thought that deal didn't look a goer, so he was making other plans, and he would question the unsuspecting agent about possible office accommodation for his business. He would also make it quite clear that he had the necessary funds in his own right. That should hurry Ernie up a bit.

It was three o'clock in the afternoon and Marina was engrossed in going through all her records looking for suitable contacts in many markets, in connection with the promotion of Far Horizons' business. She was feeling optimistic and encouraged. After all, it was only a relatively short time since she had built Chirrup up, so her information was largely up to date. She happened at that moment to be perusing her wealth of information on Singapore, when her mobile rang. She had its ring set to the opening bars of the Archduke, that always put a smile on her face and a tingle up her spine.

"Hello."

"Hi, Marina, it's Ethan Samuels here."

"And Dan Abramski. You're on the speaker."

"Good to hear you guys. Are you on, then?"

"Subject to all the caveats and seeing this place and going through whatever else you can tell us and all that stuff, like terms and conditions, we're on, yes."

"That's great. Send an e-mail with your preferred dates and come on over. We'll put you up and we can settle everything there and then."

"We'll do that. Oh, Dan has something to say."

"Marina, I will be bringing my girlfriend over. Ruth Friedman. Can you put us both up? She's a hot shot, pretty high up and important in Guzzle on the development side, so she knows all about you and Douglas. I think she might just be for you too, so I'll send her CV over as well. No obligation, but this could be a piece of luck. We are getting married next year by the way and I haven't worked on her about Far Horizons. She's her own man and I leave that to you if you want to give it a try."

"Sounds good. I look forward to your e-mails."

Marina got up and danced off to her kitchen. She looked briefly in the American fridge-freezer and then pulled out a bottle of Badoit. She poured herself a large glass of sparkling mineral water with mountains of ice from the ice-maker. She returned to her work with a lightness of tread. This Guzzlette might be just what I need. Hooray for networking.

Ernie put the telephone down with a crash and then shouted, Bugger, Bastard, Shit, Fuck, Cow, Bitch. His lawyer had just informed him of the latest broadside from the other side in his divorce case. He was up against the full force of Fender Griffiths, the toughest people in the divorce business. Theirs was a barrel you didn't want to find yourself looking down.

An hour later Mr Worrell-Smith, his property advisor rang.

"How are things Ernie?"

"Bloody awful, don't ask. What can I do for you?"

"I had as you know a meeting with Mr Dominie, the American. My advice is to grab his arm off, he's already searching for other places, I know that, because he told me and wants me to do a search for him. I did tell him that I couldn't do that because of a possible conflict of interest, which he accepted, but he will get someone else to do that. This guy doesn't hang about. You should also know that he has the funds necessary, it transpires that he sold a hi-tech company to Guzzle last year, so he isn't messing about, and he's crawling with money. My advice is sell and get the best price you can. The big house is going nowhere, so it can only get worse, which does your stables no good at all. I think this man is a godsend, until he wakes up. That may happen yet, and he may work out for himself that the stables are really a white elephant."

"Is that your advice then?"

"I'm sorry to say it is."

"It never bloody rains but it pours. If that is your considered advice, I had better take it. You don't think he has some scheme up his sleeve that we haven't seen, do you? I mean, why would he really want it? What have we missed? Do you suppose the County Council are up to something? Can you find out on the quiet, then come back to me? If there is nothing, I suppose I shall just have to sell. Get out of it altogether."

Ernie put the telephone down and settled in his chair, then lost himself in thought and miserable reflection. A volcano can lie harmlessly dormant for millennia and more, then suddenly it transforms itself and all around it bursts into a flaming inferno. That's bloody well exactly where I am now. That fucking Florence Lee, bloody Flo who I used to love and bloody well even married, fool that I am, has turned out to be a real piece of shit. And all because I caught her out with her knickers off. It wasn't even me that got caught, as far as I know she never knew about that even though she makes up lies suggesting that I was on the romp somewhere. Quite funny, that, I suppose, but life is fucking hell at the moment. How can a sweet-as-pie little girl turn into such a poisonous dragon? Such a snake and a tart? Gives a new meaning to go with the Flo.

Ernie ground his way through the next couple of days and was glad to have Mr Worrell-Smith back on the line, he hoped with some good news.

"Ok, what did you find out then?"

"I did my best, but nobody that I spoke to had any thoughts about Dale. It seems they all prefer to keep it under the carpet and forget about it. I got the impression that they hoped it would just go away, and government or some other fairy godmother would take care of it. None of the people, two actually, that I spoke to had any interest in talking about it. They seem as though they simply can't be bothered. I'm afraid we've drawn a blank there, Mr Shelton."

"Just my luck, it seems. Twenty twenty-three is not a good year. Let's hope twenty twenty-four will be better. The sooner it comes the happier I shall be. Three more months of this dead bloody year."

CHAPTER FIFTEEN

Douglas got Derick and Marina on the audio-box and spoke to them both.

"You there? Listen. I have just had Ernie Shelton on the line, he will sell, and it's for a snip, so I've said yes and I've got Sleeman Goodhart and Meyer working on it immediately. We had a bit of horse trading back and forth, but I knew straight away that he was beaten. That's why we have got such a good price. Bob Strindberg is acting for us because he is the one who knows how to deal with government and local authorities and other odd fish. He's already bashed off an e-mail and had an answer to confirm everything. If we get the big one, we'll need him, so I thought we could get used to each other on the stables. He will go like lightning too, which is important because we don't want to risk Ernie going off the boil. I gather through the grapevine that the divorce is getting nasty, too."

"I hate to take pleasure from other people's misfortunes, but that's how the world works I'm afraid. Well done."

This was Marina's token to decency. Derick came in.

"I hope that means we will be able to get Far Horizons up there soon then."

"It should. There isn't really that much to do, and we won't yet have to fix the whole thing apart from smartening it up a bit. We shall only be using a small part to begin with. Derick, you must choose the bit you would most like for Far Horizons, and we'll all fall in with that. At least we will be able all to be in the same place and things should go more smoothly. We'll get the outside spruced up too, first impressions are important."

As the year tailed off into Christmas and twenty twenty-four loomed up before them, there had been to-ing and fro-ing with Gerald Grantham. It appeared that the government was keen to get the Charter idea going and his interest had been noted. The County Council had tasked Mr Dewthorpe formally with negotiating a sale of the whole Old Dale Park Estate to Mr Dominie and his associates. They had put out feelers to the usual suspects and aroused zero interest from any other quarter in buying the place. Mr Dewthorpe and his fellow Councillors had no idea of what the prospective buyers wanted to do with it, and regarded themselves as having been lucky, clever even, to have ended up talking to Mr Dominie. They had not checked whether or not English Heritage had been involved in some scheme, and there was little likelihood that they would make that connection. Douglas, however, had taken the temperature in that quarter and got an answer that was encouraging. Nothing final, but an indication that the plans for a Charter establishment might be a good idea and they looked forward to receiving details later should the sale go ahead. That was the most you could hope for at this stage.

Back at Newton Street, Stan and Ethel were waiting to go into the Auction Rooms where their Chinese pot was about to be sold. Adam Brandridge was on the rostrum and the room was hushed. He gave a reasonably full explanation of the item he was about to sell, but Stan thought he could have said more. It sounded to him a bit brief and rushed, but of course he understood, since Mr Brandridge had explained it to him, that the catalogue had gone out to a wide population of collectors and dealers, and it had been fully exposed with excellent photographs on the internet. Nevertheless, the apparent paucity of the introduction was momentarily a worry to Stan.

A brown coated figure appeared on the floor in front of the rostrum holding the pot up for the potential bidders to see. Ethel, though she loved the idea of it, thought it just looked like a pudding basin, no more. Stan wriggled to the front of his seat. He was truly staggered to see the estimate that they had put on it. He knew what the estimate was because he had agreed it, but to see it printed under the full-page photograph of the thing amazed him. It confirmed his view that the world was topsy-turvy and had gone mad. Who on this Earth would pay between one hundred and eighty thousand pounds and two hundred and thirty thousand pounds for this old bit of rubbish?

Mr Brandridge stood up straight and announced,
"Who will start me off? One hundred thousand?"
Pause,
"Seventy five thousand?"

Another pause.

"Fifty thousand? Thank you, sir, I have fifty at the back of the room. Sixty on the net. Seventy in the room. New bidder in the room, eighty. Ninety on the net. One hundred and twenty on the net. And thirty on the phone. One hundred and forty in the room. It's against you sir. Thank you, one fifty in the room. One hundred and eighty on the net. Two hundred on the phone. Two twenty on the net. Two forty on the net. What have we in the room? Thank you sir, two hundred and fifty thousand pounds in the room. Two hundred and seventy on the net. Two hundred and eighty on the phone. Three hundred on the net. All done? Three hundred and twenty in the room. Three forty on the net. Three fifty on the phone. Are we all done? Three fifty for the first time. Thank you sir, three hundred and sixty in the room. Three seventy on the phone. A new bidder on the other phone, three hundred and eighty. Four hundred on the net. Four ten on the net. Are we done? Four hundred and ten thousand pounds for the first time. Pause. Four hundred and ten thousand pounds for the second time. For the third time four ten? Sold for four hundred and ten thousand pounds."

Stan had worked it out that they would get about three hundred and sixty something after commission. The buyer would have to pay just over eighty thousand on top of the hammer price, in commission. That means that Brandridge's got about one hundred and thirty thousand pounds out of this little escapade. He thought he was in fairyland, but never mind, they were a huge amount of money better off. He had a joke for Ethel. He'd been to the kitchen shop in his lunch hour at work and bought a pudding basin. He had left the house after Ethel, saying he would lock up and he would then catch her up. In fact, he had stayed back to put the brand-new pudding basin in his little piece of handiwork in the corner of the sitting room. He wasn't going to say anything, just wait until she spotted it. Then he'd give her a huge kiss.

When they got home, they sat in the sitting room and just flopped with a sense of unreal delight that it had all gone so well. Ethel spoke.

"Darling, shut your eyes."

Stan prepared himself to receive a piece of cake or a biscuit or something of that kind. Ethel rummaged in her basket, the one she always carried even when there was no need for it. She pulled out a brown box.

"Here, darling, for you."

She handed him the box and he opened it gingerly. Inside was a brand-new plain pudding basin. Stan roared with laughter and just said,

"Snap,"

He pointed to the little corner cupboard in which the other pot stood proudly to attention. They both leapt up and embraced like young ones. Ethel shed a little tear and Stan wiped it away, and after that Ethel put a kettle on.

"I've got some chocolate suggestives, would you like one?"

While all this was going on, Derick had taken time off to search for a flat. He desperately needed to be out of Newton Street and on his own. Now that he was being paid a decent salary, he was able to do something about it, so he started by going around the Estate agents to see what lets were available. He was not used to the new state he found himself in, where he had money in his pocket and more in the bank. He was frankly horrified by the cost of renting even quite meagre accommodation. As he entered the premises of one of the many agents he was visiting, his mobile rang and Douglas was on the line.

"Look, Derick, there is something that I had until now completely overlooked. It is so obvious that I can't think why I didn't get onto it before. First of all, you have got to get a driving licence, we can't have you dependent on your bicycle, you must learn to drive and the company has got to find you a car, all in short order. The other thing is to find somewhere for you to live. And that needs to be done quickly too. Again, I can't think why we didn't think of this before. Why don't we turn a decent bit of the stable block into a good sized flat for you? It won't be needed for offices for quite a time, and it would give you time to get on with more important things. What do you say?"

"I must admit I hadn't thought of either of those things in connection with the stables. The answer has to be yes to both. Like you I can't think why it didn't cross my mind before."

"Good, that's settled then. Let's all meet up there and sort this out, meanwhile would you get fixed up with the driving? Oh, and don't forget, the Americans, Ethan, Dan, and Ruth are coming over at the weekend. We'd better make a plan. D'you mind coming over here?"

"No, I'm on. Could someone pick me up? I won't have a licence by then."

They went up and explored the stable block to choose premises for Far Horizons and for Derick, the rest not at this moment being a priority. The place was big and extensive enough to be able to provide good space for both, and they chose to put the two parts to be renovated at opposite ends of the main building. Office would feel like office and home would feel like home. Work was started immediately and was scheduled to take two months. They should be in by the end of February and Douglas had succeeded in negotiating penalty clauses for lateness. This was unheard of by conventional contractors at this level, and they were pulled up short by this inclusion, but nevertheless agreed to work under those conditions. The stable block resembled an ant hill as workmen beavered away at all hours.

This year was going to be an election year. What a damned bore, that always disrupted things. The PM had done a decent enough job, they thought, to get back in. Thank God Brexit was history and our old friends had welcomed us back as trading partners; without that it could have been rough. And what a relief that the EU had finally given up treating us like a conquered country and we had pulled off a perfectly good trade deal in the end. Under the wire at the last minute. The cheek of it and the absolute stupidity of thinking that they could get away with treating us like supplicants. Memories had been short; without us, they would all have been speaking German by now, we were the ones who got them all out of the shit, but in international affairs there's no such thing as gratitude. If anything, we are resented. Good riddance: well, they damn nearly had done for us under Mrs Floppy May, but by great good luck the wheel had turned, and we hadn't looked back. Every nation had been struck by Covid, so relatively we were all in pretty much the same boat. It was now behind us thank the Lord, until the next time.

Back in November twenty twenty, Donald Trump had been returned, much more easily than the press in England, and even the American media, would have had you believe. How much of life is chance and how easily it might have gone the other way. By sheer good fortune, the UK had managed to negotiate a very satisfactory trade deal with America, getting over the chicken and chlorine and the steroid-fed beef debacle by agreeing to let them both in, but insisting that the products when resold in the UK would be obliged to carry clear labelling of an agreed prominence stating those facts. To the great relief of the whole nation, the government had cancelled all involvement of Huawei in the creation of the G5 network and had thereby eliminated the danger of their infiltrating the UK security systems. Better to take Chinese displeasure on the chin than to risk the national security and the relationship with America in that area. China however continued to scare people, particularly after the disclosures connected with Coronavirus and its escape from China. There had also been a lot of humming and haa-ing about the Chinese involvement in the new nuclear facilities. Fortunately Rolls-Royce had been commissioned a few years back to come up with their proposals for a number of small scale reactors spread around the country instead of a small number of monstrously large Chinese ones. This had gone a long way towards revitalising Rolls-Royce and had shown itself to be a better plan. And all British too.

The Far Horizons team thought that this moment may well be very good for the growth of the business. Overseas trade was in good heart and growing at a healthy rate, while supply chains for such industries as the automotive business were being repatriated to the UK from China and other low-cost areas. Having been badly caught out recently, the importance of this was now well understood and companies were sitting up and taking notice.

The General Election took place in the early summer, and the Conservatives got back in with an increased majority. The PM had very wisely listened in the past to his Chancellor and lowered Corporation Tax and had also, to pacify his grass roots supporters, reduced Inheritance Tax and Capital Gains Tax. The effect of the latter was to make it noticeably less difficult to raise money and a huge relief was felt in many quarters as business began to show all the signs of enhanced and fruitful activity. At long last Broadband was now available at a good speed throughout the land and working from home had as a result become the norm, following the experiences in the Covid lockdown. HS2 had been cancelled and the resultant losses swallowed, so that crucial lines of communication could be constructed in the North, connecting East with West, and Scotland had not been forgotten. In Scotland the Scottish National Party under Naomi Pike had peaked and was losing support, much to the gratification of Westminster. The south-west had gained a complete dual carriageway from London to Penzance, and the railway had been electrified, so the west country, which had supported the Conservative Party in the last election, continued to do so. Because these changes had been initiated a few years back, there had been time for the beneficial results to be evident, especially in the north, well before the date of the election.

Far Horizons had been in their new offices for the last six months as summer twenty twenty-four took hold with an August heatwave. That was unusual, August generally being windy and stormy. Derick had passed his driving test; not with flying colours, but on the second attempt he had scraped through. He was now driving an electric-powered Mini, and fast becoming an old hand. The new flat felt like home, and he had somehow taught himself to keep the place tidy. He was very proud of his abode and it was large and well-appointed enough that he could use it on occasion for private business meetings. Since the approval of the Charter scheme, work had started on developing Old Dale Park. It was not controversial to tidy up the site and refurbish the outside. Approval had not yet been given for the alterations on the inside, but there was every reason to think that they would get their plans past English Heritage, if for no other reason than that the government was firmly behind it and wanted to see it finished and functioning. Government were giving the scheme a generous amount of financial support, and Far Horizons had bought it for a real bargain price. History did not yet relate how the County Council felt when the full and wide-reaching plans were announced. They had been trumpeted by government before the election.

The three Americans had all joined Far Horizons. They had not had to work out a notice period, all three employers had shot them out of the door at break-neck speed and changed the locks on their doors. So, they were free and had joined after a short break to recover their sanity.

Derick, though very much involved in all the deal-doing and extraneous stuff which Douglas was getting on with, was toiling daily with his permanent conundrum of Far Horizons' inner workings. It was now in a state where Marina could take it more widely to market, and she had already had some success. It is never an easy job getting the attention of potential customers who may not fully understand where the benefits would lie, and who as likely as not did not like change. Added to which, recently they had probably had more than enough change, and were beginning to look forward to a calmer and more peaceful period. Marina had undeniably got the ability to paint a convincing picture to a possible buyer, even one with limited knowledge of the field in which Far Horizons operated. By picking carefully those to whom she spoke, she was showing an impressive strike rate. She was also making progress with representation of the business at conferences and symposia and other august gatherings. The future looked promising, and the assistance of the latest three American arrivals had already born fruit. Ruth and Marina were exact complements of each other, and were a good example of two and two making five. Ethan was an inventive wizard when it came to refining and extending the system, while Dan was a market analyst of extraordinary thoroughness and persistence. He was experienced at keeping his eye on what the competition were up to, and all of his work made Ruth and Marina's life a great deal more effective and brought results faster than otherwise would have been the case.

It was time to find more possible members of the team, and Marina put this to the others. Who did they know? Who was reputed to be good? Any developments in the competition which might put some good people their way? Names came up, research was done, but as yet no ironclad progress. You had to keep this

103

drive up all the time, opportunities occurred rapidly and randomly and didn't stay around for long. Vigilance was the watch word.

A couple of days later, Ruth was rung up by an old colleague from her Guzzle days. Did she know that they were now on the Guzzle radar and being watched closely? The friend, a girl called Seely Unsworth, let her know that she might be interested if Far Horizons were on the hunt for people. Ruth thanked her for the information and asked her to e-mail a CV to her at home, and she would find out what the position was. She said she would keep it to herself, nothing would get back to Guzzle or anyone else. She wouldn't even talk to colleagues here until she had seen the CV and got Seely's permission. Anyway, she told Seely that she would put her in touch if and when it looked as though it might work. Ruth put the telephone down. She knew it damned well would work. Sure enough the CV arrived that evening late at home and it read superbly. Knowing that San Francisco would still be alive and doing, she rang Seely at home.

"Seely, thanks for the CV. I like it and I know that it would be worth a meeting if you felt like it. Marina, you remember her at Guzzle? Marina would fly out to see you there, or you could come here. By the way, it's a lovely place. I'll watch this space, can I show this to her?"

"Thanks, yes you can. I'll wait to hear then. At this stage either way, here or there, would do. Let me know."

"I'll get straight on with it. Hope to see you soon. Bye"

"Ciao."

Ruth got on the line to Marina.

"I've got some news for you. D'you remember a girl at Guzzle called Unsworth?"

"I do."

"Well, she rang me today and she would like to talk joining FH. Is she any good, I've got her CV which I can e-mail over to you. It looks pretty damn good to me."

"I remember her, she's called Seely isn't she?"

"That's the one."

"Shit hot piece of work. I'll get her. Thanks."

Marina made a note of the telephone number in San Francisco and rang it straight away.

"Hi, this is Marina Slade-Knox from Far Horizons, is that Seely?"

"I am Seely."

The upshot of this conversation was that Marina got straight onto British Airways and booked a first class return to San Francisco for the next weekend, two days' time. She sat down and poured herself a couple of fingers of bourbon, then dialled Douglas.

"Douglas? Hi. We've caught a fish. I'm off to San Francisco on Friday night. I'll e-mail you the CV now. I know this girl from Guzzle days. She's shit hot."

Seely was another of the marketing movers and shakers at Guzzle and was exactly what Marina needed. The trip to San Francisco was followed the weekend after by her coming to England to take a look. Seely smelt the unmistakable scent of an opportunity to be in at the ground floor of something interesting. She also thought that she could lay her hands on a few more real performers in the business. She knew a lot of people and was attentive and nosy. She knew who was where and what they did, but more importantly, she knew how well they did it. She also could sniff out the bullshitters. All of this no doubt was why there was no permanent man in her life. She knew plenty and was choosy, but not that choosy, about who slipped into and out of her bed. For her that was physical, nothing else. She didn't rate most men as conversationalists. She didn't need that, and got rid of them after the fun, so as not to waste time and be bored to tears. You couldn't beat a drink and a good book. Especially after a damned good bonk.

CHAPTER SIXTEEN

Seely joined and immediately the pace quickened. The original team thought they were pretty quick, but this new girl Seely was supercharged. The collective feeling was good and invigorating. Seely was a success from day one. She had that fortunate characteristic that no one can cultivate. You either have it or you don't. Everyone liked her and was automatically on her side and wanted to help. Lunch at Far Horizons tended to be coffee from the exotically magic bean machine that they used, combined with things like tiny salads or charcuterie, or anything expensive that hardly nourished the body at all. This almost non-existent repast was eaten in ten minutes in the office, usually while running through papers, or maybe accompanied by a telephone call. As many hours as were needed to keep ahead of the game were worked every day. There was no clock watching, neither was staying late for the sake of it regarded as a virtue. Everyone could be sure that all would do what had to be done and none would shirk. This wasn't the kind of outfit that had any room or inclination to shirk. The whole crew had an insatiable appetite for their work and a steely determination to make it work. Not just work but succeed in its ambitious intentions and exertions.

The team arrived at eight o'clock in the morning, and there was a ritual opening of the post. This day memorably was Tuesday November the fifth. A letter arrived addressed to The Chairman. As it happened, they didn't really have a Chairman. The nearest to that would probably have been Douglas, but none of them claimed or wanted the title. There were more important things to worry about. The letter had caught their attention, and there was a general feeling that it could be suspect. It was passed back and forth between them like a letter-bomb. Finally, Marina said.

"Here, give it to me. What a wet lot you are."

She snatched it and tore it open.

It was from the London office of the New York law firm of Scravitz and Spears. That sounds sinister was the thought of all present. Douglas piped up,

"Go on then, what does it say?"

"Well, let me read it first. It's quite short, but I think it probably stinks."

Then after a pause, she continued,

"It stinks all right."

"Go on."

"It's from Guzzle's lawyers. Basically they say we are contravening their rights on two counts. One is pinching staff, the other is infringing their international patents."

"Just what we need. The staff thing is quite bogus, we and the ones of you lot who came from Guzzle, Ruth and Seely, all satisfied ourselves with the top corporate people at Sleeman Goodhart and Meyer's American office, also in New York, that we were kosher. And we were kosher."

"What about the patents?"

"We're going to need further and better particulars to contemplate that one. I can't think that we are in any difficulty at all. This is a typical try-on. These big outfits like to scare the little boys, but my bet is it won't work."

"All of you, who would you like to take this on?"

A chorus of,

"Douglas, that's one for you."

"Right," said Douglas. "There'll be blood on the floor at Scravitz and Spears. And at bloody Guzzle if I have my way."

Douglas grunted in an animal sort of a way and grabbed the letter held out by Marina.

"I'm off to get in touch with Sleeman's and have a word with their patents man and whoever else he offers. I'll get a decent idea of how serious this is."

Derick asked,

"What do they say they want from us? What is the danger here?"

"Cessation of our business and one hundred million dollars as well. They are going to have a lot of whistling to do, mark my words,"

With that, Douglas stormed out and went back to his own office.

He spoke first with Bob Strindberg.

"I know this isn't your bag Bob, but who is your guru on international patents? We are under attack from Guzzle and I have a letter from the London office of Scravitz and Spears in my hand, which makes outrageous accusations and demands. I'd like to speak to whoever you think I should talk to, now if possible."

"Ah, Douglas, you need to talk to Henry Staveley. He's your man. And he knows Scravitz and Spears as well. And if I'm not mistaken I think he's had dealings with Guzzle too. I'll transfer you. Hold on."

Douglas drummed the table as only a pianist can. He waited.

"Mr Dominie? Perhaps you could e-mail the letter to me, but what is the gist of it?"

Douglas read it out and as they spoke, he sent it off in an e-mail. The quick reaction of Henry was that these big companies toss around rude letters and writs like snowflakes. It must scare some people into action, or they'd give it up. He confirmed that he had had dealings with both Scravitz and Guzzle before and that we should not at this early stage be worried. Most of these encounters get nowhere in the end or are settled out of court. No, don't worry now. I'll be in touch as soon as I've had a look. I shall need to ask a few questions, but I will do all that by e-mail, so don't lose any sleep over this."

Just after that time, the final approval for the creation of a Charter City establishment came through. Douglas had become impatient about the time this had taken, after all, by now this is not a new idea and there are several either being done or in train. He was anxious not to miss the boat, he needed to get the best participants. They were to enclose a fifteen-hundred-acre square site around the house and outbuildings and were permitted to convert the main house and associated buildings into office and laboratory spaces for a number of tenants to be discussed. The whole thing was an area about the size of a large RAF station. A good size. Outline permission had also been granted to put up buildings in certain locations within the perimeter. They felt sure that if it succeeded, they would get the necessary detailed permission to extend. It was quite a tall order at this stage to fill such a large area as the house and its accoutrements, let alone anything beyond that. The refurbishment and reorganisation of the accommodation in the main house had gone out to tender and the contract had been awarded. The unanimous advice of those to whom Douglas spoke was to use a good-sized firm. The project would take a bit of management and a lot of time and money could be lost if the job was taken up by a less than efficient firm. As with the stables, Douglas had insisted on penalty clauses wherever he could get them in. He enjoyed this sort of thing and was good at it, but primarily he was driven by the urgency arising from external developments.

Derick had settled into his new quarters and was by now getting used to the enormous change in his life. The transition from "then", in Newton Street, to "now", in Number One, The Stables, Old Dale Park had been so great that he was in a permanent state of disorientation in this connection, though this was not the case in any sense in his new business life. In that respect he was as a duck to water. Stan and Ethel had declined his offer of a home in the same place, saying that they wanted still to be in the town and to have neighbours and the buzz of urban life going on around them. They had paid off their mortgage and found a slightly larger house in a more prestigious part of Macclesfield; it was in Prestbury Road with three bedrooms, two bathrooms, and a couple of reception rooms downstairs, with a lavatory and wash basin in a small room off the hall and a kitchen that was modern and convenient. It was the kitchen that had sold the house to Ethel, and Stan was just delighted to fall in with the plan and enjoy the increased space and the privacy. There was off-street parking and a single garage. Stan also found that the garden was becoming more and more important to him as his knowledge and experience grew. He continued his work at Stevens's because that was very much who he was. He loved his work with his machines, Stan was entirely a hands-on person. And finally, he had bought a family car, determined that he would do the maintenance and the servicing himself, even though none of his experience had been in that direction. He concluded that if he could do his work at Stevens's, he could do the work on his second-hand BMW hybrid. This particular point had still to be proven.

Derick, in a quiet moment, pondered his extraordinary and rapid progress through stages in his short life that most people either never experienced or had to wait a lifetime to see. And what a story about the Chinese pudding basin. As an aside, he thought that the new pudding basins, now stacked one inside the other in their special corner, were every bit as elegant, or ugly, as the original had been. How fortunate that the Pitt-Curnows, or rather Lady Sylvia, had given that old thing to Mum. Derick had never liked his name, he thought the name Derick was very ordinary and he now contemplated consigning it to the rubbish dump. He had been christened Frederick, and he rather fancied being called Freddie. It was somehow more humorous and welcoming than plain ordinary Derick. He also thought that his surname could do with updating to tip the hat to Lady Sylvia and her pot. How would Bilston-Pitcurnow sound? Or maybe just Pitcurnow? One word not two. With his rise in life had come a new confidence, and young though he was, he had the steel determination of the strongest. He would henceforth damned well be known as Freddie Pitcurnow. That was that, who else's business was it other than his?

At the next get together of the FH people he announced,

"You've got a new colleague as from today. Derick Bilston has evaporated and I give you Freddie Pitcurnow."

Marina came in,

"Bully for you, we only get one kick at this cat, welcome Freddie Pitcurnow."

That was that bar the bit of paper, the deed poll. He soon saw to that and charged ahead as Freddie Pitcurnow. In fact Freddie didn't even have to concern himself with the doing of this. Bob Strindberg took care of that and didn't even send a bill for the work. It even felt a bit different. A lot less Newton Street and a good bit more Old Dale Park.

Marina's further comment was,

"This is the moment to do that, because you haven't been out facing the market, so your previous name is not yet known where it matters. The new name seems to me to sound better too, so I'm entirely happy with it."

The others chimed in with their agreement, thinking he can call himself what he damn well likes, but better to do it now rather than later. Good for Freddie. Nobody thought that it would be necessary to go out publicly and announce this change, because as Marina had said, we'd caught it in time. This item closed, they went on with the important FH business before them.

The assembled company then turned to the matter of the day's post. A letter from Sleeman Goodhart and Meyer enclosing a new letter from Scravitz and Spears was in the pile before them. Henry Staveley's covering letter said that this was just more guff, but that they were doing their best to turn up the heat. An action to claim compensation jointly and severally from the shareholders and the Company was now declared and was about to be under way. Their real desire was effectively to close the place down. This missive was a letter before action, and it was also accompanied by an attempt to demonstrate further and better particulars. Henry's view was that the less we did and the more time we took to do it, the better. Their case in his opinion held no water. Let them spin wheels which would have the added benefit of keeping our costs down and theirs up. This was simply a heavy-weight try-on in Henry's opinion.

No one disagreed with Henry's assessment, and the two ex-Guzzlers confirmed that this was normal practice and they should lose no sleep over it.

Freddie's voice had over the recent few years become distinctly mid-Atlantic. This was hardly surprising since all but one of those working at the Stables were American. Even the cut-glass Marina Slade-Knox had influenced the change minutely, having subconsciously and unintentionally polished some of the sharper edges off Freddie's speech.

Freddie had continued to grow a certain amount. He was now a little thicker set and his height had increased to just under five foot nine inches. He was certain that he wasn't going to get any taller now and was pleased to have grown through the midget stage. He had become a good-looking young man, and through his demanding activity he had also become a good and attentive listener and therefore conversationalist. His earlier admiration for Marina had diminished not the tiniest bit, but he had been careful about letting this be seen or known. He was a believer in softly softly catchee monkey, and he had become practised in that dark art. In the intervening years he had taken his dress in hand and looked the perfect English gent with an American

111

sparkle. None of this had been lost on Marina, who, when she thought about it, did her best to dismiss any speculation. This she did with success, so she was not openly distracted. But she had quietly and consistently come to realise that Freddie might well be a good catch. Her view of men had not changed significantly, she still thought that from her own experiences they were hardly worth the candle. But a little corner of her active mind continued to recognise that Freddie was an exceptional being. With such a strong-minded and determined individual you had to be careful. Marina was within limits being careful. And Freddie too was being careful. Watchfully careful, though.

Marina walked through the now elegantly furnished FH office to where Freddie worked, and knocked on his door. He liked to keep his door shut the better to concentrate since he could not stand interruption when he was in full flow. At this moment he was in full flow and shouted,

"No, later."

Marina walked back towards her desk. How that one has changed. Getting quite human. She reflected on his strong features and authoritative voice, then turned her mind with some difficulty to her forthcoming conversation with an agency in Silicon Valley in what would be first thing in their morning in San Francisco. She returned to her desk, which was in the open by the others because she liked to be able to throw ideas back and forth across the floor. Luckily the others fell in happily with this quirk of hers. They quite enjoyed the stimulation it encouraged. However, they all knew not to disturb Freddie. She called San Francisco.

Silicon Valley had come up with some good news. There had been an encouraging response from there to the offer to be considered for a pitch in the new Charter City at Old Dale Park. Some good names had shown interest, including a range of technologies, including nuclear fusion and battery technology. There had even been a tentative enquiry from a firm that researched linear electronic flight at super hyper velocity. Apparently this science had advanced dramatically in the last year and looked to those entitled to express a view on such esoteric matters, as though it might be approaching a serious breakthrough. Marina smiled,

"This is bloody flying saucers again."

Then she reflected. There is so much evidence of this kind of thing. Something like this which was absolutely unlikely and impossible to believe made it onto television four years ago in the UK. Good God, only just over a century ago there was no such thing as an aeroplane and look around you now. Never be surprised, be analytical and open-minded. Why else would I be doing all this work on FH?

Freddie chose that moment to open his door and look over towards where Marina sat. She looked up. Freddie waved as if to say come on in. That is in fact what he did say, adding

"I'm sorry to have been so rude, sit down and tell me what's going on then."

Marina instinctively patted the back of her skirt, then sat down opposite Freddie.

"I've had a good morning. People are showing interest in the Charter City scheme at Old Dale. I feel quite encouraged."

"That's good. If we can't get something going, it would be quite a white elephant, but I think personally there is every reason to hope it will go well. After all, there's a whopping great tax advantage, and these hi-tech concentrations create their own momentum don't they?"

"Well, that's exactly why I am so excited. Look, business aside, I was wondering if you would feel like coming over to my place on Sunday for a proper Sunday lunch? English style. A change from all this American stuff. How would that be?"

Marina had got it off her chest, but atypically she had waffled on much more than was her wont. She regretted the momentary lapse into excessive ordinariness. She hated ordinariness with a vengeance.

"What a lovely surprise, I would love to do that. I am collecting my new friend, can I bring her too?"

Oh Good Lord, what have I done? What the Hell do I say? How can I have missed that Freddie has a girl? Dunce, bloody dunce. Damned fucking stupid cow.

"What a good idea, what's her name?"

"Thanks. She hasn't got a name yet, she's the best girl in the world of her kind. She's a proper hunt terrier Jack Russell bitch with proper long legs. I wouldn't ever have a male one. Like people."

They both laughed.

"Let's try and think of a name. We always had those at home, I love them to distraction. The name needs consonants and to be short and sharp I feel. Don't you think so? You don't want to look a pill when you call her."

"I agree, you hear so many silly names. One syllable and unmistakable, I agree, good snappy consonants."

"Like Bang. You could have three, Bing Bang and Bong."

"Thanks, Marina, I shall look forward to Sunday lunch very much. By the way, I will have a cage in the back of the car for my little friend."

"Fantastic, that's good. I might have to get one of those, they are the best thing aren't they?"

Both Freddie and Marina were relieved and excited to have got this moment behind them. Well done her coming up with such an invitation. Freddie confessed to himself, I wasn't going to do that just yet. Ever perhaps. Bloody good spirited girl that one. Don't go and fuck it up Freddie my boy.

Freddie was very hard pressed this week, as always, problems were elusive things. Well their solutions were. It will be good when we can fill out the tech side a bit more. At the present number of bodies Freddie's life was becoming very stretched. He quite understood that the total priority at this moment was to get out into the market with what we do know already works and does the trick. But I can't afford to go to sleep on the development side and more high-level help was crucial. This question must always be addressed, without it the company would melt like a block of ice under the heat of the competition. There are cleverer brains than mine and more of them out there beavering away. You can't let up the tiniest bit, boy.

The hours and the days ticked by like lightning. The weekend was upon them in no time, and before you could say it, Sunday was here. Freddie had picked up his new love, and he had called her Bong. Bong was white all over with a tan penny at the base of her docked tail, and a black and tan mottled head. Her ears were speckled with little grey-brown dots. She had long legs and would eventually be twelve inches to the withers and twelve inches from there to the base of the tail. She would weigh in at twelve pounds. Perhaps Marina would get a Bing and a Bang.

CHAPTER SEVENTEEN

Freddie pulled out all sorts of pairs of trousers and shirts. Tie or no tie? No tie.

Shoes. Dark brown Gucci maybe? He picked a pair of mahogany coloured brogues. She's English remember, not an American. Freddie felt he was running ahead of the pack, out there beyond where he had wanted to be. Get a grip, there's only one chance with this, and I've ended up here before I was ready. No you haven't, get on with it. He heard Mum's voice, just be yourself. Oh God, I'd better get some flowers. Nowhere is open now. What about the supermarket? If you go there they'll look as though they've come from there and will be drooping and probably dead by tomorrow morning. I know, go via the garden centre and get her a potted plant. What kind? Don't know, ask the attendant.

The telephone went. He rushed to pick it up,

"Hello,"

"Freddie, it's me, Marina, I'm afraid I have got a terrible gyppy tummy and a sore throat and a temperature, can we have lunch another time? I am so sorry."

Pause, then she continued,

"I was so looking forward to it. Have you named our little friend?"

"I am sorry and disappointed, yes please, we must do this when you are better. My friend is called Bong. I am hoping you might get Bing or Bang or even both."

"Ha, ha. I am so sorry, till next time, bye."

Freddie sat down, terribly disappointed. He picked up Bong and chatted to her, confiding in her, telling her his real inner feelings. He was dreadfully afraid that he loved that girl Marina, whatever love means. He couldn't get her out of his head and he wished that there was something he could do while she was unwell, anything to make her life easier and more comfortable. But there was nothing he could think of. Mum always brought grapes, but I ask you, what would she do with a grape right now? No, there was nothing. Bong chose this moment to pee down the front of his clean pale blue shirt. Oh bugger. He changed back into his normal clothes and put Bong on a piece of newspaper that was there for the purpose of house training her. In one leap he had gone from ecstatic to lethargic. He took some nondescript pre-packed things from the fridge and sat at the kitchen table and ate them. He was not very hungry and was now thoroughly disconsolate. He decided he would take Bong for a walk in the park later: he put some chocolate drops into a bag and slid them into his coat pocket as future bribery material. He pulled the ring on a tin of London Pride, then sat and enjoyed its comforting flavour. Finally, he set off for a walk with Bong. She was on one of those leads which extend to about fifteen feet, and she pulled all the time. Terriers did that, and it was a hard habit to break. That would be a task for later, not now.

He was bored and fed up. On Sunday it was to him as though the Almighty had pulled up the drawbridge. The newspapers were of little interest to him, too much paper saying too little of any consequence, although since he hardly read the things he was not in a strong position to make this generalised assertion. Nevertheless, Freddie was irritated by all the food, drink, travel, and gossip. Things no one needed to know like how to make an omelette without eggs and what some Prince or other was doing with himself, and no doubt with others, in Hollywood. All rubbish to Freddie. He couldn't be bothered with these acres of worthless newsprint, his sympathies lay with the trees. But the papers were needed at the moment for Bong. So, since they were there, he read bits of them. In today's effort was a curious article which briefly occupied his attention. There was a big class action in America which the business news said was ominous for Guzzle. He read on. The numbers being tossed around were in the billions. Telephone numbers, but that should occupy their minds for a bit, maybe take the heat off FH. For ever with any luck. He had heard from one or other of his ex-Guzzle people that all was not roses at the old firm. The context in which they had referred to it was that Guzzle executives believed that they were being left behind in some areas undisclosed. That could only be good for FH.

Eight o'clock on the dot the next morning saw Freddie in his office helping the new week to steam into action. He thought what a relief it was to know that the place was full and buzzing with energy and hard deep toil. Brains may be silent, but the feeling of exertion was palpable, food and drink to Freddie after the intense vacuity of the weekend as well as the heartfelt disappointment of the cancelled lunch with Marina on the Sunday. He was going through a sheaf of short notes which told him what progress had been made by the spearhead of the busines, the development team, during the previous week and in which directions. He was gratified to see that the scope of FH's offering was broadening and deepening. Time to get some more heavyweights in to sharpen up the technical side. Thank God the revenues were starting to flow, and flow regularly. Marina, whose bout of illness had been quickly cured with Imodium and paracetamol combined with rest, had clearly been going hammer and tongs with her group and had been achieving good success. Thank God. If that were to dry up, it would be Good Night Vienna in no time, but mercifully that didn't appear likely. Marina and her henchmen, or properly her henchgirls, had brought home the bacon. Bloody well done. Funny she hasn't said anything about our Sunday lunch since she got back. I do hope she hasn't forgotten. Perhaps I ought to take the onus on myself and find somewhere to take her to lunch as her host before she goes off the idea completely. If she hasn't already. He got the website up for La Reine Claude, a two star Michelin restaurant a few miles away. He decided to make a booking for next Sunday. If Marina couldn't make it, he could always cancel and rebook. After doing that he felt better, now all he had to do was ask her. Blood was now up, and he picked up the internal and she answered. Momentary jitters, then after an unnoticeable pause,

"Marina, how are you fixed for lunch with me this coming Sunday?"

"God, can you cook?"

"No, nothing so grand. How would you like to join me at La Reine Claude this Sunday lunch time?"

"I'd love that, thank you, I shall look forward to it. Have you got a minute? I want to talk to you about Guzzle?"

"Yes, any time, I can talk any time."

"I'll come right over."

Marina came in. Oh God, Freddie thought, it's only Monday morning and this girl looks a dream. Nothing flashy, nothing cheap, just a bloody miracle. He took a grip of his wandering mind and greeted her in as matter-of-fact a voice and manner as he could muster. Underneath that mask, he felt uncontrollably drawn to her, and his words came out as quiet and benign, not as he had intended at all.

"Look, Freddie, I hope you've got a minute?"

"I have, go on."

"Well, I'll have to start with a little story. There was a boy, a Stanford lawyer, frightfully good-looking, athletic and pleased with himself. His name was Grant Davenport I think. He ran and jumped and kicked things around and generally thought too well of himself for his own good. He got the hots for me when I met him at a do in San Francisco, a friend's drinks party. To cut a long story short, I got groped and belted him across the face. Actually, I gave him a black eye."

"That's a good start, I can't wait to hear the rest."

"Well, there wasn't a rest really. He went around in dark glasses with his tail between his legs for a bit, I heard. I never saw him again or heard a squeak from him."

"And?"

"I had a call from him on Friday. He's now in the legal department of Guzzle and he tracked me down when he heard I was at FH. These people know everything, it's their business. He's probably still wounded enough over that old débâcle to want to show me how big and successful he is now and what a catch he would have been. That's all disgraceful speculation on my part, but the point is he got in touch, not by e-mail or messaging, but by phone."

"I'm intrigued, please continue, this is fascinating."

"Amazingly he felt moved to tip me off. I mean about Guzzle going for us, He said they had bigger fish to fry at the moment, and if we played our cards right, they were of a mind to drop the whole thing. He also said we were now well and truly on their radar."

"So what does it mean, play our cards right?"

"He sent me a draft from his own private smart phone, giving the gist of what we should do. It boils down to a letter of apology

119

to the Chief Honcho at Guzzle promising to be good little boys in future. I think we ought to run it past Henry Staveley at Sleeman's, and if they agree, do it."

"Well done you. I like the story, and I agree. See what Douglas says I should, but I don't think there are any dodgy wrinkles in it, do you?"

"No, I don't, I agree, I'll do that."

Douglas was tickled by the story. Nothing so strange as folk.

"Wheels within wheels, eh, Marina? What would we do without you?"

"Thank you, kind sir. Will Henry Staveley deal with it and send you something to sign? You'll have to be Chairman again Douglas!"

"Yes, we'll let him do it, I think. I think it shouldn't look like a lawyer's letter. It obviously only works, I suspect, if it is private between the two top dogs. A face saver. And it does seem they have quite a headache to cope with at the moment. Who knows? That could be good for us. It could suit us rather well in the future to be on their radar."

Henry came back the next day with a short letter, taking up about three quarters of a page of A4, saying as near to nothing as possible, but which sounded utterly to the point. Henry had had a bit of fun and had consulted Roger's Thesaurus here and there. Americans like long words, and Henry had dug a few up for them. It read as though it had been wonderfully officiously and officially constructed by a very contrite Chairman, but still managed to say absolutely nothing. A good lawyer earns his corn, thought Douglas Freddie and Marina when they read it. In about a week's time a vacuously cobbled together answer arrived from Mr Kowalski, Guzzle's head legal counsel, enclosing an equally ill-considered handwritten note from the Top Boss, Mr Halkidopoulos, as though assuming sovereignty over FH. The matter was now, thankfully, closed.

Douglas sent a bottle of Veuve Clicquot to Henry Staveley, hoping that might short circuit any bill he could be thinking of sending. He knew that if that little game worked, the missing bill would simply be added to that for the next occasion when Henry's services were needed. This little game had worked before, but every move had its riposte.

For Freddie, as for Marina, the week was too short for all they wanted to achieve. Marina and the others in her section had had a good week. The market appeared to be taking to FH, and growth was now recognisably encouraging. With all the costs, and the start-up burdens, to say nothing of the dead time it had taken to get the show on the road, they were still a good way from showing a profit, but cash flow had been vastly improved recently and there was every hope that a small profit might appear next year. They had not yet had to go to outside equity investors for further finance. To cover peaks and troughs the bank had been surprisingly helpful. A by-blow perhaps from Coronavirus, which mercifully had by now virtually disappeared. As hoped for, the hot weather when it came had helped suppress the virus, and the Oxford and UCL vaccines had been miraculous. So far they had done the trick, long may that last. There was even the faintest evidence that China was feeling a little chastened, it having been proved beyond doubt that the spread had been due to their negligence and dishonesty. China was now in a feverish state. Their one great fear had always been chaos, and after the bullying of Hong Kong and its partial relocation to the UK, the population of China had grown braver and more restive. The world knew that imprisonment and execution were still common there and could well be on the rise. China, as always, was a space to watch. Many an industrial company had cut its dependence on China for its supply chain. Long gone industries had returned to Great Britain and to Europe. Great Britain had become the favourite relocation destination because of the favourable tax regime and the good trade relations with large parts of the world. Europe was still struggling and muttering about level playing fields, but nobody was really listening to that old song anymore. Since leaving the EU, the City had increased its dominance of the European financial sector. There is much that no government can influence, but the outcome following the stormy years under the burden of Covid-19 having turned out to be more satisfactory than had been feared, the sun shone on the United Kingdom.

Stan and Ethel were still amazed and delighted by their windfall, and they understood why Freddie had changed his name. They were glad to see that the name of Pitt-Curnow had been perpetuated, because they had on the one hand liked and admired Lady Sylvia and been grateful to her for her gift, and on the other hand they had appreciated the fact that a family with whom their own family had been so closely associated, had been revived and that the name was still heard in these parts. They were amused that Freddie had amalgamated the name into Pitcurnow, just to make the difference and make it sound less exalted and a bit simpler and more ordinary than it had been before. Their new house was a revelation. They now had peace and quiet and space, and they had a garden too. Stan had become a serious grower of vegetables and enough cut flowers for Ethel to be able to keep the house fresh and pleasantly scented as well as being full of colour. Stan still loved his work at Stevens's and remained a wizard at complex machining. It had been his life and he saw no reason to make any changes on that front. It was a relief to him that Ethel was now able to be a lady of leisure and did not have to do cleaning work to make ends meet. Even though she had enjoyed much of it, the pleasure deriving from being appreciated, she was quite happy to be able to do things for herself and to read more. She had always been an adequate cook, but now she took a real interest in it and had become quite expert. Nothing fancy, but everything good and wholesome. The new house with its drive and parking space was perfect for his parents. The brand-new pudding basins were in pride of place in a little alcove each, either side of the fireplace in the sitting room. Stan had made them. It was one of the first things he did when they had moved in.

In such spare time as he had, which was very limited, Freddie had kept up with Peter Braithwaite and the Probus Club. The difference was that now they had asked Freddie to give a talk on the genesis of Far Horizons. This had caused Freddie a good deal of worry, but he did eventually put together a talk which appeared to have been well received. Freddie wasn't sure about that and made a mental note that he wouldn't let himself in for such an ordeal again, and he didn't.

CHAPTER EIGHTEEN

Old Dale Park Holdings had been set up by Douglas and Marina with Freddie as an equal partner in order to accomplish the purchase of the huge and important white elephant from the County Council. It had been funded by Douglas and Marina with a share capital of five thousand pounds and a vast secured loan to cover the rest of the substantial sum required to complete the deal, provided equally by Douglas and Marina. Later, a monumental chunk of money was provided by Government and that very same Council when the full plans had been approved and work on the Charter City had begun. To fund the development of the City, business partnerships were formed with a number of property development companies which had been granted conditional tenure on various specific parts of the overall package, in order to accomplish separate objectives related to a range of hi-tech activities. This arrangement had worked well and development had proceeded apace, with new firms now joining the mass concentration of intelligent toil in the Charter City which had resulted from Douglas and Marina's initial efforts. Freddie had participated by taking up his share of the five thousand pound share capital, using funds provided for him, as part of his recompense for kicking the whole thing off, by Douglas and Marina. This enterprise had run itself successfully since the beginning, thanks largely to Douglas's close attention to it and his punctilious monitoring of its activities. Douglas had seen it as important that he should keep the details of the day to day supervision of this largely in his own court, to avoid disturbing or having a deleterious impact on FH itself. In that, he had succeeded.

The office was its usual self, an imitation of an intellectual pressure cooker. In other words, it was steeped in normality when Douglas summoned Freddie and Marina to his quarters in the stable. They had questioned the need for this and both had said that they couldn't afford the time, would the weekend be better? Douglas had said emphatically that this would not wait until the weekend and would they please get their asses over in double quick time. In order to oil the wheels, he had added the vital information that they would not be disappointed by what he wanted to tell them.

"Hey, you two, come on in and pin your ears back. I won't beat about the bush, we have struck gold, us three!"

The initial feelings of irritation in Freddie and Marina evaporated immediately. There had been occasions when good news had come in, but gold had not yet been struck. Marina spoke,

"Don't fuck about Douglas, we are busy little beavers, just what is all this?"

"Come on Douglas, out with it."

Freddie felt equally impatient, but now on tenterhooks.

"OK, we've had an approach, as near as you can get to an offer, from just about the biggest noise in the business to take us out of ODPH. I get the impression that they are likely to be talking huge very grown-up sums of money."

A chorus of Good Gods rung out.

"Who, how much and when?"

"Stateside Charter Investments, a subsidiary of the Bunker Musk Foundation are the bidders. It wouldn't surprise me if there was a king's ransom in this. After this, I will call Bob Strindberg at Sleeman's and get him lined up. And James Struther at Siegel Dornhof and crank him up too."

Marina and Freddie left with tails high in the air. Douglas dialled up Bob.

"Bob, we've had an approach from Bunker Musk, their subsidiary Stateside Charter Investments, to take us out of our investment in the Charter City, to buy ODPH outright. Will you please stand by to do the spade work? This looks like being a big one. They've got Armour Benson doing the accountants report and Lowman Paine Lyons are the investment bank. Do you know these people?"

"Yes, I do, Douglas, and of course we will happily act for you, well done. I think I ought to get a letter out to the other side without delay. Will you send me theirs and I'll get to work. Yes, I've worked with Armour's and with Lowman's, I know them both. Tough but straightforward, at least we won't have any of that ghastly New York trickery, these are decent firms, both of them. Are you using Siegel Dornhof?"

"Yes, James Struther will do this one for us. We think he's pretty thorough and you don't easily get the better of him."

"I agree. He's very clever, nobody's fool."

"OK, thanks Bob, I'll get hold of James Struther now and we'll get the show on the road."

"Douglas, I'll e-mail my proposed letter to you first, then the next thing you'll hear from me will be a response from the other side. I will make sure you get everything as it happens. All this sounds good to me, talk to you very soon."

Douglas sat back in his chair for a moment to think about this. Time to ring James Struther and brief him.

"James? Douglas. Look, we've had an offer for the Charter City, to take us completely out of ODPH."

"The whole thing?"

"The whole thing. Will you act for us? The other side has instructed Armour Benson to do the accountants report, and Lowman Paine Lyons is their investment bank."

"Well, well, well. That sounds like a big one. Should keep you in Veuve Clicquot for a bit. Yes, of course I'll be happy to do this one. Those firms are both sensible, so that's a relief. This should be pretty uncomplicated as to value too. It all depends on how many and what sort of participants they get. As I understand it, you have already got a good many first-class names who've agreed to take up a plot, haven't you?"

"We have, and in quite a wide range of hi-tech activities. We've even got flying saucers!"

"That should be worth a bit!"

"As soon as you think the time is right, I leave it to you to get in touch with Stateside. Doubtless they will put you in touch with Lowman's and Armour's and then it's over to you to take it at whatever pace you think the thing demands. You know we've got Bob Strindberg at Sleeman's acting for us doing the legals. I think you know all the players. Over to you my friend."

"Thanks Douglas, I'll be in touch as soon as I can see what the plan is. We could have this one all wrapped up pretty quickly if the other side see it that way. I can't think that they would have any reason to delay things, they don't I am sure have year-end problems or anything like that. I can't see that there are serious tax implications in this either. An outfit like Bunker Musk doesn't mess about. Talk to you soon."

Documentation was all prepared in double quick time. There was not a great deal to be negotiated other than the actual price to be paid. There were no special conditions attached to the sale, it was basically plain sailing and without contention. It was quite clear to Stateside that the sooner they got this done the better. ODPH was constantly looking at potential new takers and each time they signed one up, the unknown element in the deal was reduced and the price stood to rise. Stateside wanted to stop all that by doing the deal quickly. They couldn't sensibly try to restrict the gaining of new business, the only way to pin the price down was to complete the deal.

A completion meeting was to take place in the City offices of Siegel Dornhof, under the chairmanship of James Struther.

The three partners all went down to London and booked into the Savoy ahead of the meeting in the City at two o'clock the next day.

The meeting was the usual theatre in the presence of both principals, one party on the left of James, the other on the right, his assistant Noel Lincoln on his right, beside him, and the two firms of lawyers and accountants at the end beside their clients. By this stage there really wasn't much more to do than to sign the pile of papers which would govern the future of the new company. There was little scope for ceremony or grandstanding, and the whole thing was done by four o'clock. At that time, the table was cleared, and soft drinks were brought in. Toasts followed, and people began to look at watches. The room was empty by five o'clock and everybody went his own way satisfied with a good day's work.

Back in the bar at the Savoy, Marina spoke first.

"Holy shit!"

Freddie simply said,

"I thought you were pulling our chains? When you said billions I thought that's more noughts than hairs on my head!"

"I didn't actually say that, but as you have discovered today, you're on the right lines!"

Marina spoke again,

"Come on, Douglas, I know what we all need. Let's order the Widow and talk about this."

The party went into the River Room and ordered one of the best dinners they had ever had, then they started to reminisce.

Someone had told Douglas at that meeting in his office when he announced that Stateside had come in with an offer, to get over to the fridge and liberate a Widow.

Douglas had needed no more prompting. He went over to the imitation Louis XIV fridge freezer and set free a beautiful bright yellow Magnum of Veuve Clicquot. There was much talk about everything and nothing. The unreality of this very real development had not yet turned into belief. They were, all three, in the euphoric state of disbelief, and much abject rubbish was talked that morning. Not much work was done that day by the three principals.

A month or two later, after they had returned from their trip into the City to complete this extraordinary deal, Freddie knocked off at six that evening and drove over to his parents' house at Prestbury Road.

Ethel answered his ring at the door and gave him a proper motherly hug, but only after she had let him in and closed the door.

"Dad is just back from work and he's having a bath upstairs. Stevens's are very busy these days you know, he is so pleased. He loves to see what he makes, he says he picks it up sometimes and wonders at how machine tools could make such things, they start as just plain lumps of metal he says, then something magical happens. And he's behind it. I've never known him happier. We miss our dear Derick though."

"Freddie."

"Freddie."

Stan came down looking fresh and clean, a discreet trail of Old Spice following him into the room. Maybe not dressed up, but looking smart, and he'd shaved too. They must be going out thought Freddie.

"Dad, very smart this evening, are you going out tonight?"

"It's Mum's and my wedding anniversary, and we are going down to the Albert and then on to a nice little Italian restaurant for a celebration dinner. We are here for a bit though. It's lovely to see you."

"I mustn't keep you. But I wanted to tell you the latest news. We've sold The Old Dale Park business to an American Foundation for telephone numbers, and I have got an indescribable amount of dosh for my share. I hardly like to talk about it, it is such a windfall, and honestly, for what?"

"Well, I'll be blowed. I don't know how you do it, son, but well done. Yes, very well done, mystery though it is to me."

Freddie tossed around in his mind the life that his father and mother had led. He admired the deep sense of pride that his father felt about his apprenticeship with Rolls-Royce and qualifying as an engineer and becoming a much-respected practitioner of his skill. And for doing such a tangibly practical thing with his life and succeeding by his own demanding lights. He then cast his mind critically over his own gargantuan achievement and saw it as something so small compared to the progress of his parents against strong tides and steep hills.

For some unaccountable reason, Freddie had a bottle of champagne still in his car. He had bought it at the supermarket when he had dropped in to buy some fruit and a few nibbles to have with drinks and had spotted the champagne which was on offer. He had bought half a dozen bottles and all of the shopping was in the car, as he had forgotten about it. But he remembered it now and left the room to fetch a couple of bottles.

"Where's he gone then? That was a bit quick."

"He must have gone to the car, silly. He'll be back."

Freddie returned and handed the two bottles one to each parent. He then did a thing he hardly ever did, after giving his mother a hug and a kiss, he went over to Stan and put his arms around his father's neck and gave him a heartfelt kiss on the smooth cheek.

His father stiffened with momentary embarrassment, then he relaxed and gave his son a warm hug in recognition of the pride he had come to have for his brilliant son. At this point there could have been tears of emotion, but though there was emotion, there were no tears.

CHAPTER NINETEEN

After a long and gruelling haul, the weekend finally arrived. A walk, leavened with anticipation and excitement, and the training of Bong, got Freddie through Saturday. When Sunday came, he spent time deciding what he should wear. Nothing too smart, but something to show that he had made an effort to look a credit to Marina without in any way overdoing things. Being an admirer of finely engineered articles of quality and artistry, he had bought himself a rose gold Calatrava watch by Patek Philippe, with a brown crocodile strap. He enjoyed the knowledge that minute and superbly made cogs and springs were contained within its slim circular case, and kept perfect time for days, weeks, on end. And at the first sign of success a year ago, he had also bought a pair of dark brown brogue shoes from John Lobb and company in St James's Street in London, having heard of them from Douglas who was also a customer of theirs, along with Napoleon and Queen Victoria. He had had to visit their shop and be measured for the making of wooden lasts of his feet, which had impressed him greatly.

Freddie walked out into the courtyard where his electric Mini stood. He looked at it and was suddenly truly aware of the fact that should he wish to do so, he could now order an Aston-Martin. He was surprised to discover that this realisation failed to cause the rush of adrenalin and blood to the head that he might reasonably have expected. He wasn't at all sure now that he actually wanted one. There was nothing wrong with the Mini. With his appreciation of complex concepts combined with artistic appreciation, he was beginning to incline towards an exotic and rare classic car of some kind. Something better made than an Aston-Martin. He had over the last few years quietly picked up a bit of detailed knowledge of some of these outstandingly interesting beasts. He looked at his watch. Half past eleven. Too early, it would take twenty minutes to get to Marina, then half an hour to get to La Reine Claude, and he didn't want to be early for either. He wandered around the beautiful house for five minutes, then returned to the Mini and unplugged the electric lead through which it was kept topped up with electricity.

Freddie had prevailed upon his cleaner to look after Bong for the day. She had professed to be delighted with the arrangement, although Freddie wasn't sure that she appreciated the amount of work that might be involved. Bong was only partially house-trained, and that was a bit chancy. Kylie, however was undaunted and gave many a cuddle to the much-loved terrier. She probably gave her a few other things too, which Freddie would rather not know about. He was determined that she would be well trained and not lick or jump up or steal food. So far, he was more or less on track and believed that soon he would have the most obedient Jack Russell in Derbyshire. Kylie was a real boon and took this role on more and more as time went by. And Bong didn't appear to suffer, she wasn't getting fat and she didn't misbehave. Much.

As the greyhound in pursuit of the hare, Freddie raced off to Marina's home. He put the wheel over and went slowly up the drive. He turned the Mini and parked it to one side of the steps which led up to the beautiful oak front door to the even more beautiful Manor House belonging to the off-the-scale-most beautiful-girl-in-the-world.

Marina had heard his approach and met him as she opened the door and stood there looking down over the drive. Freddie's heart missed a beat. She was smartly but light-heartedly attired in a colourful silk top over a dark and full linen skirt. Minimal jewellery, the Vacheron in evidence. The whole picture was crowned by her spectacular and natural-looking hair. No help was needed with the colour, but the arrangement had, he suspected, required skill. She smiled and came down the steps to meet him.

Both were delighted to see each other, but the stage of kissing on meeting had been studiously avoided by both, in fear of starting something which they might later regret. Freddie opened the door of his car for her and she got in with accomplished elegance. Freddie, rather clumsily he thought, found the belt for her and she snapped it shut. So far nothing beyond a brief but friendly greeting had been attempted by either party. Clearly nervousness was in the air. Freddie reminded himself of the dictum about softly catchee monkey and got into the car and they drove away.

The drive to La Reine Claude was on twisty country roads with dry stone walls either side for most of the way. The sun shone on the Peaks and the fields were a vibrant green, beauty was about on all sides. The faintest scent of something stimulating and exotic began to circulate, given a shove by the air conditioning. One day he would ask her what it was. Marina spoke,

"What fun this is. I feel so good to be your Veiled Lady this morning, this lovely clear sunny morning."

"I am looking forward to seeing the Reine Claude, they say it is pretty good, so let's hope this is a good day for them. I just want to say how lovely you are looking, you are an absolute picture."

Freddie turned the car and put it next to the way in, then got out to let Marina out. He noticed that she had waited for him to come around and had not leapt out unaided, which she could have done with unruffled ease, but she was enjoying what was beginning to feel like being wooed by a truly well-mannered young swain. No formality, but no undignified familiarity either. Within, she glowed.

Having agreed to skip the bar, they were shown to a table by the window with distant views of the countryside for which Derbyshire is known. Freddie put her where she could see out and admire the view. This she noticed too.

They were now seated and in no hurry to bombard each other with conversation, a calm had descended, aided by the quiet un-showy decoration of the dining room. There was French grey, there was gilding, and there was lovely fresh crisp linen napery at each place. The cutlery was not the modern stuff that is so unbalanced and wants to slip out of your hand or fall off the plate. This was civilised and of excellent quality. Freddie spoke,

"I think it would be fun to push the boat out a bit, don't you? If you're not embarrassed by it I thought this was a great opportunity to have a bottle of the Dom, would you join me?"

"Would I? I would."

"I happen to know that he has tucked one away for us, so let's get hold of it. Fizzy water too?"

"I'd like that."

The Sommelier materialised silently beside them and Freddie asked for the Dom Perignon that he had ordered during the week. And a litre of fizzy water too.

Marina spoke,

"You know, I do love France, it is such a wonderful place and makes me feel inspired. And their turn-of-the-century painting, their music. I really love France."

"The pleasure is before me, but I have always understood that it is a special place. I think I've heard it said that everybody loves his own country, and France."

"Benjamin Franklin I think, but it seems to be so true. When you think that we used to own most of it years ago, it makes you sick to have lost that, don't you think?"

"And what a sadness to think that we have been enemies on so many occasions. I am determined to get to know France, and I've been told that if you want to get on with them, it pays to speak their language too."

"I'm not much good at that I'm afraid. I remember that as children we were embarrassed to speak it, we had to distort our faces in very un-English ways and that just made it embarrassing really."

"I know, I never really got to grips with it either, probably for the same reason, I think I reckoned it made me sound and look a fool, so I didn't take it seriously."

"My little experience of French people is that they are absolutely fine and have more respect than we do for formality. It's Monsieur and Madame, not this Mate and Old Cock business."

The two of them enjoyed their outstanding bottle of champagne and the meal gradually passed through such wonderful delicacies as escargots, homard, and crême brûlée à la maison. Freddie went through the carte des vins with Marina and the sommelier and they chose a Château Margaux and a bottle of Sancerre. They went right through the menu to cheese and coffee. Both of the bottles of wine were more than half full at the end of the meal, and the Sommelier recorked them and gave them to Freddie in a little two-bottle holder as they left.

Freddie noticed that the bill was more than he would have dared to contemplate a few short years ago, but this day's value had been priceless.

On the way back to Marina's house, Freddie thought to himself that the best thing to do was to say goodbye at the front door and get back ostensibly to pick up Bong, but in reality however viewed, not to push his luck. He thought the lunch had gone magnificently, but he didn't want to try to take things any further now, better let it all sink in and hope that Marina had enjoyed it enough to initiate a return match. Catchee Monkey.

He dropped in on Kylie on the way home and picked up Bong in her little cage lined with what looked like a week's worth of newspapers.

Marina went into the house and ran straight upstairs to change out of her glad rags. She had a long hot bath with some smelly stuff which she poured into the steaming water, and then she lay there reliving the most enjoyable lunch she had had for ages. She turned the facts of the last few years over in her mind. First I meet a teenager who is a genius, but a schoolboy and I am a working woman who has already made a pile of money. Then I find out that this boy has done something so amazing that I put real money, lots of it, into his business, Then I find out that he's a bloody good egg and now a grown-up man and I think I'm falling in love with him. I could almost be his mother. Well, no, it's only eight years, and that is nothing. Don't make a fool of yourself. When I am fifty, he will be forty-two. So? Her rapier sharp mind had gone all woolly. Look on the bright side, you haven't had any luck or fun with men, you know they're mostly bastards, but what have you found here? The reality is amazingly, even at my age, that I have no idea what good sex is like. They always refer to it in books and you hear about it all the time, but what is good sex? I've always found it mechanical, painful, and messy, so what do I know about it? I don't suppose Freddie knows much about it, he probably has only ever pulled his own plonker. Well then, we could work all this out together with no preconceptions. We could I suppose, but how can I be sure of that? You can't, but it might just be worth a try. Better than some sex-mad bastard who just wants a fuck between his many commitments. I really do not want any of that. She smiled as she recalled her father's expression for unremarkable and disappointing people and things. SOSTA. Seen one, seen them all.

Marina finally got out of her bath as the water began to show signs of cooling again. She had already added some more hot water once, but this time she decided to get out. Just look at the time. The sun would be over the yard-arm soon. She slipped into a pair of silk pyjamas and put on her silk house coat over the top. She wasn't expecting anyone to call, and if anyone did, she would ignore them.

Freddie put Bong on the grass in front of the stable, hoping that she would perform, but nothing came of it. Better keep an eye on her then. Things happened without warning, so he had to be on his toes. He mooched about in the flat doing nothing in particular. His mind was on Marina. He had found the lunch perfection, they had chattered away about everything under the sun. And she is so quick, so bright, so unbelievably attractive. I know all that from business, but as a person, outside all that corporate stuff, she's in a class of her own, and I feel so relaxed and happy in her company, there is no stress, where in such a case there could be. This is a miracle, don't go and fuck it up. I don't know anything about sex. I've never met a girl who I wanted to get hot with and more importantly I've never met one who would give me a second look. She must have had dozens of boyfriends and she would always have had the pick of the bunch. What would she want with me? Seriously, I mean it boy, what the hell would she want with me? I am at least not a midget any more, but I am pretty small. Yes, but you're taller than her aren't you? Yes, but by how much? Anyway, what has that got to do with it? She did at least put up with me for lunch and I'm a Chinaman if she didn't enjoy it. Or is she just like that with everybody? No I don't think so, she's quite impatient actually. Enough speculating. Do nothing for a bit, watch some telly to get your mind off all of this. Countryfile, Antiques Roadshow, then blessed bed. Just don't dwell on this miracle creature it will drive you off your head if you go on like this. I know. Give it a crack next time, see what she does if you give her a kiss. Why not?

With that Freddie calmed down a bit and sat down and put the TV on.

Stan and Ethel had not yet opened the champagne that Freddie had brought; they were going to save it for an as yet undisclosed special occasion. At the weekend they were still revelling in their outing at the beginning of the week on their Wedding Anniversary. They both recalled and talked about their celebration dinner in the Italian restaurant, Ciao Miao, which was meant to mean Hello Pussycat. An attempt at humour by the ex-ice-cream maker who owned the place. They had both had spaghetti carbonara followed by tiramisu. Ethel was no good at making up her mind what to have, she preferred to follow Stan's lead. He was a little irritated by what he judged to be a shortcoming, but it was their wedding anniversary, so this wasn't the moment to pick her up on it. Stan was a devoted husband and he was very proud of the wife he loved so much. Now it was time for bed, they had watched the Antiques Roadshow, and after scrambled eggs it would be time for bed.

Marina woke in the middle of the night and the idea of telephoning Freddie crossed her mind, but she quickly thought better of it, though she would have liked to have been able to talk to him. She was restless and in a slightly agitated mood. Further sleep didn't seem likely.

She and Freddie met at eight o'clock in the morning. Monday morning, the beginning of the new week. They were both praying that everything would be normal between them and that nothing had occurred or happened to take the shine off their Sunday lunch adventure. Each was a tiny bit wary, but as soon as they met and started discussing the agenda for the week, everything settled down and all was well. There was the added fact, which the lunch had given rise to, which was that each now felt immeasurably easier with the other. Not that there had been any difficulty or stiltedness before, but the lunch had dropped some oil into the works and what had always been good was now better.

Freddie's door was open and he could hear Marina sounding like her old self. Brief, concise, to the point, engagée, intelligent and dominant among the other strong characters. She had the gift of not appearing to be at all bossy, but nevertheless getting her own way most of the time. This was generally because she had a knack of being right as well.

CHAPTER TWENTY

Such were the forces of restraint in each, that a full fortnight passed before Marina invited Freddie to join her on Sunday for dinner at her home. This time it was for the evening and not for Sunday lunch. The small point of detail was not lost on Freddie, and he gladly accepted. There had been no frosting over, it was simply that the office had been extremely busy and neither of them wanted to push the thing too far too fast and in so doing to push it out of shape. Their earlier lunch together at La Reine Claude had made such an impression on both that it didn't need to be dusted down and given a polish every day. The two of them knew where they stood in each other's esteem and they had no desire to risk over-doing it. So they played it caringly cool. But cool can also be warm, and this was such an example. Some of the more observant in The Stables had noticed the slightest signs of a change in the relationship between Freddie and Marina, but it had not yet reached the status of office gossip. Freddie and Marina were determined that it should not, and each subconsciously understood the subterfuge.

During the intervening two weeks, Marina made another of her frequent visits to Silicon Valley, on a recruitment drive and on a mission to get the name of Far Horizons out in front of important players in the market and set up a future sales campaign. To attend to the detail of this effort, she would depute the task to her by now well-honed team. When it took place, she would be there but it would not be up to her to work out all the details. She now had very competent staff whose task that was, and she intended to do no more than check their plans out and introduce the opening session and sum up at the end. Even these two formalities would in the near future be conducted by her well trained and experienced people. The outward looking face of the business was now predominantly female, and the technical engine room was fairly evenly split between males and females. Rewards were exactly equal, Freddie and the other two being committedly insistent on this point. Nothing else made any sense and there was no discussion on this non-subject. While she was in San Francisco she would do a little poking about and talking to people in the know, about the position that Guzzle was in at that time. Time spent in reconnaissance was seldom wasted. That was a favourite dictum of her father, and it was a well-tried military principle with which Marina whole heartedly agreed.

On the return flight, she happened to bump into Grant Davenport, the boy she had given a black eye to all those years ago, and who was now high up on the Guzzle legal team. Marina had not noticed him when they boarded the plane. She was travelling First Class and as soon as they were airborne, she settled down in her own private corner and didn't look around at all. What she wanted was peace and a rest, so nothing beyond her own little area figured in her conscious. A figure came slowly up to where she lay half asleep and looked down. He smiled a self-confidant sort of a gesture which reeked of friendship on his terms, and said,

"Marina Slade-Knox, could it be you?"

Marina woke quickly and thoroughly from her wakeful slumber and looked at the man.

"I am Marina, yes. Don't I know you? You are....?"

"Grant Davenport. We communicated over that little débâcle Far Horizons had with Guzzle, do you remember? I was the one who got in touch with you to help sort it out."

"Of course, I remember. I'm so sorry not to have got that straight away, forgive me, I was rather dopey at that moment."

"I hope you don't mind me coming over, but I was sure it was you."

"Not at all, why not sit on that empty seat and we can catch up a bit. I am afraid I am pretty worn out at the moment, it has been a busy trip and when I get back I am up to my eyes, but it would be lovely to have a quick little chat."

Grant had noticed that Marina was wearing an engagement ring over a wedding ring, but he was not deterred. He said to himself, half of the time those are false, crack on. Grant said,

"I am on my way to London to take a look at what gives. I like to keep up to date on the gossip, and I am also on the lookout for acquisitions for Guzzle. We never stand still, and it is only by being up to speed that we can know what is going on and who is going where."

"Essential stuff, I should say."

"How are things at Far Horizons now? I hear you are still snapping up some bright cookies, the word gets around you know."

"Well, they are our life blood, aren't they?"

"Oh, that they are. I hope you won't be fishing in our pond."

"No, no, I wouldn't worry about that. They come to us, we don't have to fish in anybody's pond. Remember, you cured us of that."

"Ha, well, it's nice to see you again, and we'll keep in touch."

Grant returned to his seat and got up his tame London dating agency's app on his smart phone. In Grant's estimation and judging by his experiences with them, this agency was really an escort agency masquerading as a dating agency, after all, why else would he use it? He selected the appropriate page, put in his preferred details, and chose as exact a replica of Marina as he could find, looking carefully at the photographs pouting at him from his screen. He arranged a meeting for the next evening at the Ritz in Piccadilly, and then booked in for dinner in their main dining room for eight o'clock that evening. He also took the precaution of booking a double room there for that night just in case. You never knew, she might be something, or she could turn out to be a scrubber: the voice told you a lot, but of course you don't hear that until it is too late. Grant arranged to meet his date at the bar at half past seven. He then lay back and dropped off into a deep sleep, interspersed with extremely erotic dreams about the vision sitting a few rows down from his seat and also in First Class.

When the flight reached Heathrow, Grant made sure that he left the plane next to Marina, beside whom he walked into the terminal. When they reached their destination, he gave her his private card with his own personal addresses and numbers. This version he kept to give to what he referred to as prospects. He leant over and planted a kiss on her cheek, rather farther from the target he had in mind than he would have wished. Marina could think of nothing but the black eye incident and with a little difficulty restrained herself from a repeat of the performance.

With great relief she saw the company driver who was holding up a card bearing her name. They walked out to where her Bentley stood waiting, and as she got in, Grant bustled by looking for a cab, and just noticed her as her elegant slender leg disappeared into the cocoon of the Bentley. This pleased her greatly. Bastard.

The next morning, Marina sat in Douglas's office with Freddie and they had a de-briefing session. She was most keen to pass on the information that Guzzle were on the hunt for embryo acquisitions and that she had met Grant Davenport of the black eye, on the plane. He was the one who was on Guzzle's legal team and had helped them over the falling out, which Henry Staveley at Sleeman's had dealt with. Grant was conducting preliminary sleuthing for Guzzle. He was in London for the purpose. She added that he was still pretty obnoxious, to which Douglas said,

"Well, we may have to dangle you in front of him, you know, like dry fly fishing."

"Ha-ha!"

"No. I think we should put that to the vote. Looks like a winner, Freddie has a beaming smile on his face."

"That brooks no reply. I'm off."

With that, she was gone.

For Freddie the working component of the week rushed by at super-sonic speed, such leisure time as the job allowed went at the pace of a tired snail. He filled in with a morning and an evening walk with Bong. Sometimes she was lucky and got a lunchtime one as well. The house training was making good progress and accidents were now rare. He hoped that when she was truly civilized he might be able to bring her into the office. He could see no reason why not, provided that she behaved herself and didn't go racing about distracting people. He knew that next to Jack Russells, people were the most intelligent beings on Earth. Freddie felt he should be clever enough to be able to judge when the time Bong could join him in the office had arrived.

The five working days of the week melted seamlessly into one another and Saturday came. He decided that he would like to have lunch with his parents and felt that Bong should come too now that he had her reasonably well under his control. It was plain to see that Bong worshipped the ground he stood on and was at the same time full of beans, as well as being happy to lie with her head on forward placed front paws, resting but ever alert, to rise in one bound should action be on the cards. Freddie thought, there is no friend like a Jack Russell, only my Marina knocks you, old Bong, into a cocked hat.

Stan and Ethel were very taken with Bong, and she was even forgiven for letting go on the rug in front of the unlit fire.

"Never mind, I'll mop it up. You'll never see it on that Turkish rug, so full of colour. Lucky it wasn't on the nice new pale carpet Stan has just laid."

There was a grunt from Stan, Freddie thought more in amusement than in anger. His father was being very mellow and was genuinely pleased to see his son. And the dog. His old father had had terriers and Stan had always got on well with them. He had never forgotten having his left thumb bitten by an angry Border called Ruff, or was it Rough? But that was a long time ago and his father had always kept his terriers outside, they were very definitely working dogs and nothing more.

After tea with a Victoria sponge cake made by Ethel, Freddie made his way back to his flat in the Stables. He then took Bong out into the Park for a quick run about, and anything else that the little terrier could manage. There was a lot of running about, squirrels to be chased, pigeons made to fly, but nothing more. Freddie knew that the clever thing to do was to stay out until her mood changed and she got on with it. He sat on an oak bench and watched as the little terrier raced about all over the place at breakneck speed, then suddenly came to an abrupt halt and left a large offering on the grass. Freddie picked it up in plastic gloves and a little inside-out bag, then put it in his pocket to get rid of in his dustbin when they returned to the flat.

Freddie sat in his favourite comfortable wing chair and settled down to read the new biography of the last Tory Leader. He could just remember her, but at the age he was at the time, she had made no impression on him, so he was bringing himself up to date reading this new book written by Simeon Law, one of the BBC's reporters who had taken to writing biographies. He was in the process of writing one about the Leader of the Labour party at the same time, but the word was that it had fallen behind schedule, possibly due to diminished interest on the part of Mr Law and the publisher in that subject.

Freddie was beginning to find the biography heavy going. He was unable to understand why she had not lived up to the expectations of her supporters. They had hoped that she would get on and see to it that stuff was achieved in a reasonable time. Many of those who had been behind her in the Leadership race looked forward to the accession of a new Mrs Thatcher, but all those hopefuls had been gravely disappointed. Nevertheless, Freddie was not one to give a book up halfway through, he would grind on and finish the thing, even though the signs were that it wasn't much of a read.

How quickly time goes by. America was again in political turmoil, another Presidential Election due. Trump would then finish his second term and the world hoped for a sensible straightforward middle of the road candidate to emerge, but so far the field looked broadly pretty dud. There was a general feeling on this side of the Atlantic that nobody with any sense would stand for that job. If ever there was a poisoned chalice that was it. It was also hard to believe either that Putin still held a recalcitrant and troublesome Russia in the palm of his hand, or that China was still the unhelpful autocratic communist dictatorship that it had been since the beginning of the days of Mao, some eighty years ago. Taiwan was now under constant threat and the world held its breath. More breath was held over Russia's unaccountable support of Iran and its mischief-making and oppressive mullahs. Nothing changed. The reducing dependence of the industrialised world on Middle East oil had continued to decline dramatically, but that part of the world would always find spurious reasons to scrap amongst its constituent countries. Now was no different, except for the fact that their collective clout had reduced considerably and would continue to do so as oil was gradually supplanted by cleaner alternatives. There was in this country an increasing feeling of distaste and the necessity to do something about it, in connection with the harsh and inequitable way that women were treated in the Middle East, Asia and above all in parts of Africa. With the constitution of the United Nations so woolly, that organisation had shown itself to be even more toothless latterly than earlier.

There must not be a soul on Earth who could not see that it was an ineffectual farce, nothing more. And of course it was suffering from the fact that as a result of its make-up, the lunatics were running the asylum.

Though both were still very young, Marina and Freddie were deeply concerned about the lot of women in Third World countries, in their own country even, as well. And they both considered the relentless population growth, again particularly in Third World countries, was one of the greatest threats that the World faced. Sooner or later the human race would run out of space and be unable to provide life-saving resources for a population which increases exponentially. It didn't take much brain to see that, but what to do? Well, that was easy, stop it. The question was, how?

Freddie's mind was racing round in circles. He had abandoned the biography for the evening and thought maybe a curry would be good. Then bed, and tomorrow he would see Marina at her house. He had the day tomorrow to get through before the excitement of the evening. Somehow, he would find a way. Possibly with the help of Bong. Beyond a doubt with the help of Bong.

He parked his Mini outside the New Taj Mahal. He got out, and the smell of curry greeted him, the faint scent of it in the street in front of the closed door. He went in and was met by the owner. Freddie noticed that the owner spoke a clear easily understood English, far better than most of the ordinary western English around about. Someone had done a good job with this fellow. He hoped the curry would be as good.

He ordered a glass of Tiger beer and half a dozen poppadums and some mango chutney, then he looked through the menu. There was no limit to the choice, but every kind of curry could be had either with lamb, or chicken, or prawns. There were lots of vegetable curries too, and he was particularly pleased to see brinjal. He was partial to aubergine. Eventually he chose a prawn jalfrezi and a side dish of sag and brinjal, he was keen on spinach too. He thought to himself that was probably a very poor choice from a gastronomic mixture point of view, but that was what he wanted. No doubt there would be laughter in the kitchen. So what?

A replete Freddie returned to the Stables and let Bong out for a run and whatever else she might choose to do. He had a torch to help him spot any result that he would need to remove, then called her and they went upstairs. Freddie put the news on the television. Why do they mess about with the times of the news on Saturday and on Sunday? Then he went to bed and soon was lost to this world.

CHAPTER TWENTY-ONE

Sunday arrived bright and sunny. Freddie was restless with anticipation of his dinner with Marina. A whole day to get through before seeing her. The normal pace at which days evaporated had slowed down to an agonising crawl. This time he wouldn't get caught out and forget the flowers. After a leisurely breakfast and a brief run for Bong, he put her in the car and they went off together to the florist in Macclesfield. He knew that they would be open because he had telephoned them earlier in the week to make sure. He didn't want his flowers to be droopy, they must be pristine, so it was important that they should be super fresh. Nothing too showy, but something good, no lazy heads or dying bits. He thought it might be the time for red roses. Is that a bit premature? You could argue this one either way and it would probably pay to know the old-fashioned code about the colour of the roses. Marina would almost certainly know that. We all know what red roses mean, but yellow is a bit dodgy, so is white. If it is going to be roses, then what is wrong with a bit of honest truth? Freddie marched confidently into the wonderfully scented florist's shop, "Bloomin' 'Eck," and picked up a dozen of the reddest biggest most scented roses that the shop could offer and which he had ordered in advance. He wasn't going to be caught out this time.

While the mood was upon him, he dropped in on an antique silver shop that he had passed on the way to the florist. In for a penny in for a pound. Who knows, they may have a beautiful rose bowl, and it would give me so much pleasure to make a present of such a thing to her. Where's the problem with that? He knew he loved the girl, it was no fantasy, it was utterly genuine, so have a look. If there is nothing, it will at least pass the time, and if there is, well, she will be a lucky girl and the truth will be out. You can't go on for ever hiding your light under a bushel.

He went a little gingerly into the silver shop. An attendant smartly dressed in a dark blue blazer and a quiet expensive tie, generally smartly dressed in a respectable way, came up to him and asked if he could help. Freddie said first he would like to have a look around. Were the prices marked? They were. He paced slowly around the shop followed by the faithful Bong. On a table, placed neatly in the centre, was the most exquisite rose bowl in silver that he had ever seen. Not tiny, not huge, just right, about seven inches high and ten inches across, with a silver grating to hold the roses fitted inside, and it was undamaged too; as pristine as the day it was finished. Made in 1807 in London by Paul Storr. This was just the thing, A George III silver rose bowl of the highest quality. Freddie was in a mood to do this and make his feelings plain. He knew it was a risk, but he couldn't go on in the present limbo of not admitting the realities for ever. This was shit or bust, but something told him that it would be a good thing to do. So he did.

He stopped and turned to find the owner respectfully behind him, at a polite distance, but following him just the same. Freddie said,

"I like this, it's beautiful. Can you please quote me your best price on it?"

"Oh, you've chosen well. It is by Paul Storr and of the best quality. 1807. I was lucky to find it, it's only been here a few days and already there is much interest in it."

He then quoted a price, and Freddie answered,

"I'll have it. It is exactly what I am looking for and will serve its purpose well, I hope."

Freddie handed a card to the owner of the shop with the words,

"I was lucky to find you here on a Sunday, wasn't I?"

"Oh, no, sir, Saturday and Sunday can be my busiest days, I take my weekend on Monday and Tuesday."

Freddie went straight back to the florist with his bowl.

"Look at this, I've just bought it. Tell me, how many of your lovely red roses will I need to do an arrangement in this?"

"What a beautiful bowl, I've never seen one so lovely. Let me think. To be on the safe side I would say you'd need fifteen or sixteen. They do of course get bigger as they open fully, but I think you could need a few more than the dozen you already have. I think I would suggest another four."

"Thank you, that is what I'll do then. Is there anything I need to know when arranging these in the bowl?"

"Not really, just remember to cut the stems at an angle and then split them a tiny bit to help them get the water they will need. There is a little sachet of white powder in with the ones you already have, open that and pour the powder into the water and stir it about a bit before you put the roses in. They should last well I think."

Freddie and Bong returned to the car with their new prizes. He put the flowers carefully on the rear seat and the exquisite bowl in its box on the floor at the back.

As soon as he got home and after letting Bong romp about outside for a little, he took the bowl out of its box and its wrapping and put it in the centre of a circular table in his dining room. It looked perfection personified. He then fetched the roses and held them above the bowl to admire the pair of treasures for himself. Stupendous. He hoped beyond hope that he wasn't about to make a fool of himself. A little still voice told him to bomb on with confidence. He wrapped the bowl carefully in the tissue, as had the antique silver man done when he sold it to Freddie. In its box and in its wrapping, it looked exciting and mysterious.

It was still only mid-afternoon. Freddie paced the flat impatiently.

He sat at the computer in his study and googled up Guzzle to see what there was on them that might be informative and new. He looked at their latest accounts and their 10-Q and was interested to see that they were doing quite well considering the blip they had had last year. An article in one of the specialised publications quoted Mr Grant Davenport, a legal counsel, as saying that they were on the acquisition trail and confident of an exciting future for their company. In the F.T., Mr Halkidopoulos the Chief Executive Officer of Guzzle was quoted saying something guardedly bullish. Freddie knew how much to aim off when assessing such entries in the press, but Guzzle were obviously in optimistic mode nevertheless.

Freddie got up on the screen the corresponding stuff on Far Horizons. Looked OK. He noticed that there was a quote which said Mr Freddie Pitcurnow was lying doggo when asked for his comments; watch out for future developments in this promising newcomer. He liked that. Nobody had asked him anything or said anything that would support such a comment about lying doggo, but he did like it. Maybe someone had been in touch with Douglas and he'd told them that I wasn't available for comment. It could be that.

He shut the computer down happy that the world had not collapsed and that all seemed to be on track. He went and sat in his leather wing chair having picked up Simeon Law's biography again. He ground on and confirmed his earlier view that it was a bit turgid and put it down once more. The clock was still decidedly at a slow walk, so he went back to his bookshelves and looked for further inspiration. For a bit of harmless levity, he pulled out Alan Clark's diaries. They were always good for a laugh. Could life really have been like that then, all those years ago? My God, how the world had changed, but he enjoyed the frivolity of Clark's writing and settled down picking pieces out of it for another half hour.

The hands on the clock edged their stately way towards the time when he felt it was right to go and have a leisurely bath and a good shave. He remembered Mum telling him to be sure and wash behind his ears. There was something deliciously decadent about having a bath at a time that was just after the end of the afternoon. He revelled in it. Better than ass's milk. Having eventually left his bath, he turned to shaving. The theory was that the hot bath would make the beard more compliant when it came to shaving and the result would be a better shave. It mattered not a scrap whether this was true or not, but Freddie did manage a good close shave and he did not make any cuts. Looking at his face in the glass, he thought he didn't look a teenager any more, he looked ordinary, normal, grown-up, like everybody else. And he was minimally taller than her too. Good feeling. Don't put on smells, he felt sure she would prefer him au naturel, without those silly smells as advertised on TV at Christmas. Time to get dressed.

Freddie went into his walk-in cupboard to pick out something to wear. He had a rather nice single breasted dark blue blazer which he liked. Not too dressy, but well cut and quite smart. A pale blue cotton poplin shirt and an Hermès tie, elegant and not brassy, finished off with a pair of maroon linen trousers and the slip-on shoes in dark chestnut leather made for him by Lobb's.

That would do. He knew she would be a knock-out whatever she wore, so his wish was to be no more than a foil to her pearl.

He emerged clad in all this splendour in time to give Bong a final run, put her bed into the car, and set off at last for the longed-for dinner with the love of his life, Marina.

CHAPTER TWENTY-TWO

At five minutes to eight the Mini turned into the gates of Marina's house. Marina was in the hall, as alert as a blackbird listening for a worm. She heard the Mini stop, then turn, and a voice say come on Bong, out. Freddie took out a large plastic bag with the rose bowl in its box inside, and an even bigger orange plastic bag to hide the roses. He put Bong's bed outside the orange bag and put all that under his right arm, in his left hand he carried the green bag containing the treasure. Bong followed. Finally, Marina heard the car door shut and footsteps approach over the gravel and then mount the steps. She opened the door.

Freddie entered and put his burdens on the floor, telling Bong not to jump up and making sure she stayed in her bed. Bong sat there like a coiled spring, her head on one side and her front left paw raised.

Marina spoke,

"I hope that's your luggage, you're staying the night."

At that, the pair of them sprung together in a passionate embrace and kissed with all the pent-up energy which was in each of them.

Marina eventually unfolded herself and simply said,

"Supper is cold. Bong you stay here. Come on Freddie, follow me."

She held his hand as though it was her last link with survival itself and steered him to the grand staircase over the black and white marble tiles in the hall.

Together they went up slowly and gracefully into Marina's bedroom.

"Freddie, my darling, I want you so badly, it just doesn't work to supress these things. Be gentle, we have the whole night."

"My precious Marina, what is there left for me to say? I concur, I love you with all my heart."

Clothes were not folded, nor put away, they lay in a progressive trail in the direction of Marina's bed which was the biggest Freddie had ever seen and the broadest that she could find. The floor was strewn with the dark blue velvet skirt, the silk top, the odd diamond peeking out of a fold, and Freddie's deep blue blazer and maroon trousers, salted and peppered with an assortment of underwear.

The session started with a long lingering embrace and many kisses, but it didn't take long to change key towards and into fore-play, during-play, and after-play, following which, it started all over again. Words were few, but expressions said it all. There was in that room no inhibition, just sheer commitment, and joy.

They must both have fallen into a deep sleep for who knew how long? They had slept with their bodies intertwined, but motionless. On waking, warmth turned again to heat, and it was not until nearly ten that they went downstairs again, this time Marina was in a silk dressing gown and Freddie had been given another similar one. He noticed that it had never been worn, it still had the labels everywhere that told you its history and provenance. Freddie thought Marina must have gone off and done a rose bowl on him.

As they reached the marble of the hall, Bong came bouncing up and jumped up on them both. Freddie tried to exercise a little discipline and put her on her bed. He went over to the two supermarket bags and handed them both to Marina. She opened the roses and was overwhelmed by the beautiful blooms that she found. And this was a girl who doesn't overwhelm. She took the box out of the other bag and slowly opened it. Then she opened the well-presented container and carefully took the tissue off. There stood the most exquisite piece of craftsmanship, true art in fact. She came over to Freddie and wrapped her arms around him and whispered over and over again, thank you.

"Shall we have some supper first and then put these stunning things together into an arrangement?"

"I think your lovely supper has waited long enough, don't you?

Marina had made a lobster salad with deft skill, and they started with half a dozen oysters each. She always thought a full dozen overdid it, so her preference was for six. Freddie was delighted with what she had prepared and fell to with enthusiasm. Marina had got hold of some unusual cheeses, and there was fruit salad with fresh mango, peach, pear, and grapes for pudding. To create this supper Freddie thought a brain must have been at some pains to get it right. Marina had started before the meal by opening an iced bottle of Pol Roger. This delectable wine followed them right through their supper, it having enough companions in the American fridge in the kitchen to satisfy all needs. Strong Greek coffee followed. No need to worry about drink and driving this evening.

After supper, they repaired to the kitchen to deal with the roses. It seemed Marina knew exactly what to do. She said her mother had always kept distilled water in a bottle, from the tumble drier, for just this purpose, and also to put in her steam iron. Her daughter did the same thing, so the pure water was fetched and the magical powder stirred into it. Then the roses were put up against the bowl to get an idea of how much to cut off, and Marina with a practised efficiency snipped them all diagonally and put a little longitudinal nip in each one. After that, she set about arranging them in the newly acquired and much appreciated present.

After the concentration of arranging the roses, she came around to the other side of the table and embraced Freddie with the gentlest and most heartfelt of kisses. Bong made a little sound in her throat that said don't forget me. Marina lent over and ruffled Bong's spotted ears, and she settled down again in her bed.

Both of them felt a happy satisfied warm feeling and they got up slowly and ambled over to the staircase. Hand in hand they mounted the elegant ladder to Heaven, and went back to Marina's bedroom. They dozed for a short while, then their passions once more roused, they became consumed with each other again. The night to both had been a privileged dream, and they felt so entirely at home the one with the other, that each began to build castles in the air. But Marina was a faster builder of such structures than Freddie, who at this stage of his life was more of a novice than was Marina.

CHAPTER TWENTY-THREE

Marina picked up the internal and dialled Douglas.

"Douglas, you alone?"

"Quite alone."

"Have you got a minute?"

"All the time in the world for you my love, come on in."
Marina slipped her shoes back on, got up, and went over to
Douglas's voluminous office.

"Come on in, let's sit over there and you can tell me what's
going on. What is this all about?"

"Douglas, I am going to get married to Freddie."

"Great Heavens, that is a surprise. Is he out there? We must
get him in and open something."

"No, not so fast, he doesn't know yet. I mean I haven't yet
told him, or rather I mean he hasn't yet proposed, but watch this
space, you'll see I'm right."

"I must have missed something. How long has this business
been a-brewing then?"

"Oh, it's quite new actually, a few weeks, that's all. Look,
what I wanted to ask you was this. I would like to take next full
week off to go down to Cornwall and take Freddie with me, is
there anything you have in mind for then that would make that
impossible?"

"Not a thing."

Douglas sat still and just breathed, then he spoke, having
substantially recovered from this golden bombshell.

"Well I don't know, usually I can sniff that sort of thing out
with no trouble, but you have stolen a march on me this time. Did
I say congratulations and I wish you both well?

"No, you didn't."

"Congratulations and the best of everything to you two. Can
I be the Godfather?"

"You'll be the first to know, and we'll certainly interview you
with a strong possibility that you'll get the job."

"Freddie's a lucky chap, let me tell you that my love. If I
wasn't a poof I'd have snapped you up ages ago, but there we

are. I am so happy for you both. Assuming that Freddie will play ball."

"We've played a bit of ball, that's partly how we both know. It will just take me to tip the thing over the edge. I'll set up Cornwall then, and give you the dates and numbers for next week, but our mobiles are as always the best thing. And don't you bloody well ring unless there is a cataclysm. Now, don't give Freddie any of your funny looks, OK? And not a word to anybody. Anybody at all, do you hear me Douglas? Silence."

"As the grave."

Marina went across to where Freddie's office was. She made sure that she was carrying a bundle of papers, it would be a pity to blow the gaff on their plans now and carrying important-looking stuff was generally a good disguise. She needed time to get things arranged and the future settled. She needed to do it her way, no lovey-dovey stuff around the office and no gossip. She would soon enough tell everybody, but not until she, she and Freddie, were good and ready. She knocked on his door and Freddie invited the knocker in.

"Oh, it's you. Come on in and sit down. What's all that you've brought me?"

"Oh, that? That's just a blind, I just wanted to look busy to anybody who saw me, but really I came to ask you about a plan I am hatching."

"What fun, what can that be then?"

"Well, I would like to go with you for a week down to Cornwall. Have a real break from all this for say a week? How does that sound to you?"

"I think it sounds absolutely wonderful. Can you spare the time? When do you want to do this?"

"There's no time like the present, as soon as possible if that suits you. Next week? Go this Friday and come back on the Sunday of the following week?

"What a splendid idea, I can't see any reason not to go. One week is as busy as the next, I agree, if we don't just do it we'll never find the time. Yes, let's do that. Your Bentley I think."

"My Bentley, yes."

"And I think I'll get my cleaner to look after Bong. She loves the good Bong as if she were her own."

As Marina passed Douglas's door on the way back to her desk, he came out and stopped her.

"Marina, take a look at this, it came in today's post, I think it may interest you."

Douglas handed her a letter, then turned and went back into his office.

Marina went and sat at her desk and took the smartly presented letter from its already opened envelope. It was addressed to Douglas Dominie and was from Grant Davenport suggesting that in the interests of understanding the market better, it might be beneficial if he were to meet Douglas and the others at Far Horizons before returning to the United States. The purpose of this would be to have a general get-to-know-you conversation and to bring the FH people up to speed on the progress that Guzzle was now making.

Marina rang Douglas,

"Good moment?"

"Yes, come on in."

"Douglas, I take this to be a fishing expedition, don't you?"

"I do."

"By the way, I had planned to take a week off starting this Friday evening, back Sunday following. Does this change things do you think?"

"I don't think it does at all, if they are serious they'll be back. I would have thought we write a polite letter saying in three months would suit us fine, what do you think?"

"I think it would be better to be quite cool but not dismissive. It wouldn't do to over-react, people like that are very sensitive to the reactions of others, that is the metier of the M&A boys. Is three months long enough to keep them waiting? What's wrong with six?"

"We must think about this, then get together, will you give the letter to Freddie? No, I'll do that if you like, that may be better since it was addressed to me. Leave that to me, I'll give it to him this morning."

A few days later Grant Davenport was discussing his European trip with Mr Halkidopoulos back in California.

"So, what did you find, Grant?"

"I met quite a few of the right kind in the UK, Cambridge is full of near misses and of course Oxford is not behind them with more near misses. Don't get me wrong, all worth knowing, but my feeling is that there isn't anything there for us at this precise moment. There may be exceptions, but I'm not completely sure yet, I'm working on that."

"Strange, I would have thought there might be something there for us, but if you say there isn't, then I believe you."

"What I am really saying is that there doesn't appear to be anything immediate there. Not at the moment, but I am sure there will be in the future. Hard to say when, they keep their cards close to their chests in the UK. But there are stirrings of interest. More later."

"What about the rest of Europe?"

"Europe's a different kettle of fish. Hard to make some of it out, and Brussels gets in the way a bit. There's some promising work going on in Germany, and France is always worth watching. Switzerland too. I think Europe is a case of keeping a close watching brief."

"Nothing else?"

"I've got my eye on a relatively new English outfit that seems to be making good headway, they're called Far Horizons."

"Do you know them?"

"I know one of the founding Directors, and I've written to their Chairman to say that a meeting to get to know each other might be worth doing."

"Any response?"

"Nothing yet, I had hoped to see them before returning here, but so far nothing."

"What makes you think they could be worth getting to know?"

"They have some interesting algorithms and are making fast headway in the market. The time to get them is when we can offer them what they would think is a lot, and before they get too big and therefore expensive."

"Didn't we have a bit of a run-in with them quite recently?"

"We did, I sorted them out and you wrote to their Chairman, and we heard no more."

"Yes, I remember. They were poaching people and we tried to get them on patent infringement. I knew that wouldn't fly, but sometimes you can scare the ones who get out of line. Didn't work, so on to the next."

"Well, they're worth some attention now. They should be treated like a nursery plant. Or at least my judgement says that would be the most beneficial way to play it for us."

"OK Grant, why not keep a weather eye on them? I agree we shouldn't leave them out there too long just to get more and more valuable. Not if we have already sussed them out correctly. I agree with you, Grant. Do that."

Grant left it another week, then wrote in friendly terms to Douglas again, saying that he was sorry to have missed them on his recent trip. Perhaps we might meet when next I am over in Europe?

As Grant wrote the letter, Marina and Freddie were enjoying a leisurely break in Cornwall.

CHAPTER TWENTY-FOUR

Kylie Sedley, Freddie's cleaner-cum-general-helper, put Bong's bed into the back of her hatchback, then bent down and picked up the slightly bemused terrier. Freddie gave the little dog a cuddle and a good tickle behind her spotted ears, and then Mrs Sedley was off back to Macclesfield, Bong looking inquisitively out of the back window at the fast disappearing master. And then, Freddie was on his own.

The electric Mini sped up the drive to Marina's house, he turned it and parked it to the side, next to the Bentley which shone in the morning sun. He then went up the steps and let himself in. Sun beamed a low flat rising light into the marble hall, presaging a fine day, and he felt at home. On the floor in a neat group were Marina's cases. Two fine chestnut coloured squishy leather bags with M. P. S-K. in gold lettering on them. He had never asked her what the P stood for. Philippa? Priscilla? Patience? Highly unlikely to be Patience, what irony that would be.

Marina having heard him arrive swept into the hall and came over and gave him a huge kiss. A mid-morning-we-are-going-somewhere kiss, not a lingering passionate one. Plenty of time for that later.

"I'll take your bags down to the car, I see it has had a good polish since I last saw it."

"Yes, a Polish polish. Stanislas in Mac does it for me."

"Tell me, what does the P in your initials stand for, what is your middle name? I've never discovered that."

"Secrets, secrets. Actually it is Penelope, but I don't much like it myself, so I never talk about it. Now, you know, my Ulysses."

Freddie transferred his holdall and his suit-bag into the boot of the Bentley, then he put Marina's elegant luggage around them, and she put in a basket which contained a picnic for the journey. This she had made with loving expectation earlier on that morning. Egg sandwiches, cherry tomatoes, fruit, a knob or two of cheese, and some oatmeal biscuits. She also slipped in a freezer bag which held a bottle of elderflower cordial made with sparkling Derbyshire water. They had both known a colleague who had been killed a couple of years ago by a drunk driver up on the High Peaks in the snow in the middle of winter. It had been late at night when the pubs were closing. Any drink while driving was verboten. Absolutely not contemplated even, by either of them.

The Bentley Continental eased out between the black and gold wrought iron gates and turned onto the country lane that would eventually link them with the motorway system and take them onto the M5. After Bristol, they continued to Exit 25 at Taunton and turned off to the south to have lunch in a sheltered lay-by at Henlade. Never was an egg sandwich more appreciated than at that point, made even better by being washed down with the fizzy elderflower drink.

"Freddie, would you like to take over and drive for a bit?"

He felt some affection for this Bentley, he had already driven it enough to be comfortable with it, and he wanted to be able to give Marina a bit of a rest. This car was truly a magic carpet, and Freddie looked forward to the next hour or so. He knew Marina would get impatient after a pause like that and would want to get behind the wheel again.

"Yes, I'd love to. Give you a rest for an hour or so. It nearly drives itself, doesn't it? I love driving it. I might even get one."

After they had done justice to the picnic, he crossed over at the gap in the dual carriageway before Thornfalcon and went back onto the motorway. He thought he would take the Bentley as far as Sourton on Dartmoor, and then hand it back for Marina to do the bit down to Cornwall. He didn't know Cornwall at all, he had only been there briefly with his parents when he was tiny in their Royal Enfield on Ethel's knee. Not very comfortable, but exciting for a small boy, and unusual. Not many of the boys in his school at the time, probably none at all, had been near a motor bike and sidecar combination.

Freddie had no knowledge of where they were going, other than to have been told its name. It was a small private hotel called Penhendra Manor just to the north of Penzance towards St Just. Marina said it was very secluded, beautiful, and comfortable and had a good chef. She remembered that it had lovely views over the sea by Land's End, across open moorland, and there were lots of good walks there. She hadn't been to Penhendra for years but knew it because she had stayed there a couple of times in the long vacation from Trinity College Cambridge with her parents. On one of those occasions it had rained ceaselessly. This time, Marina had booked a room with a sea view and a huge bed for their adventure. It was not raining, and there was a good chance that the weather might be fairly benign. By Cornish standards.

The hotel was a large version of the typical white painted black slate-roofed Cornish architecture. Nothing much to look at, but comfortable inside, so they hoped. It had a large single storey extension attached to one end, with a view over the moorland and the distant sea. This was obviously the dining room. There was a big terraced area in front of this room so that on those occasions when Cornwall chose to let the sun in, the customers could sit outside. Mostly, in this exposed position, it blew a gale.

Once they had been shown into their room, Marina decided to make a cup of tea while she thought about having a bath. As the kettle boiled, she turned her mind to other things and put the bath idea right out of her mind. She climbed up onto the bed and lay on her back, hands beneath her head, strawberry blonde hair in a halo around her face. Freddie was thumbing through the folder which had been put there for them to see what was happening in the area, but otherwise was just sitting there admiring the sight of Marina lying before him on her back. Sheer beauty. Marina swung her legs over onto the floor and made two cups of tea. The couple sat and looked at each other, brains ticked, silence reigned. Marina went over to where Freddie was sitting and took his hand. She drew him to her and they embraced tightly and passionately. Freddie looked at the bed and gave the smallest nod of his head. Marina nodded, and the next thing they knew they were in bed naked and entwined. Two cups of Earl Grey tea slowly cooled off and then became stone cold, sitting on the table by the kettle.

In high spirits but a little tired from the journey and the exertions of the afternoon, they had a bath, put on some fresh clothes, and went into the dining room, The menu looked good, they both read it thoroughly, then chose. Between them they had whitebait properly done with paprika, Coquille St Jacques, Steak

160

tartare, rack of lamb, and much else. The cuisine was remarkably satisfying and the sommelier's cellar was up to the high standard set by the chef.

After dinner, they sat in the sitting room next to the dining room and ordered a couple of glasses of Naughty Water, chatting about everything and nothing. The plan for the next day evolved into a trip to Lamorna Cove and a look at the Edwards Passmore Gallery at Newlyn. You never knew quite what to expect there, but it could be wonderful, or on other occasions it could be awful. The Kümmel Naughty Water went down a treat, and having enjoyed its flavour of anis, they then retired to bed at about ten o'clock.

By the time they reached their room, a different agenda, a variation on just going to bed, had suggested itself. Further gymnastics filled their minds and occupied their bodies. This time, after their exertions, they were finally bombed out and they turned in for a deep satisfying sleep. They slept the sleep of the dead right through to half past eight the next morning, ready for a leisurely get-up. However, by the time morning had come and had woken them fully, its arrival heralded another gentle session, and two very happy people went down to the dining room for a full English breakfast. Marina noticed too late that there were kippers, proper real brown smoked kippers, not the orange supermarket dyed ones, and she made a mental note to have a pair tomorrow.

Marina and Freddie both took great pleasure from the visual arts and particularly enjoyed the work of the Newlyn School, which is why they wanted to drive down to the south western coast of Cornwall and take a look at Lamorna Cove. This out-of-the-way place is a diminutive collection of a few small cottages and a beach, approached through lanes with high Cornish hedges, which in fact are always solid stone sided banks down there, and are not to be taken lightly. These obstacles deny evasive movement to any vehicle confronted with another having a cavalier attitude to spacing. The meagre twisting lanes run beneath arching trees, ashes, oaks, sycamores, and cast shadows in strange shapes across the tracks. Lamorna was a favourite place to paint en plein air during the hey-day of the Newlyn artists, and the effect was appealing and romantic, producing fine paintings of an impressionist nature, suggesting much, but simply constructed, with great skill in composition. They understood what to put in their paintings and more importantly what to leave out. As the Bentley navigated its way down this hazardous little track, they thought of Lamorna Birch, Alfred Munnings, Laura Knight, Stanhope Forbes, and others. Beside them was a narrow sparkling stream following the gentle slope down to the sea.

During their stay they took in Newlyn itself, a once great fishing community in the days of the supremacy of the Cornish pilchard. There was still fishing going on there, more than there had been until recently, because of the merciful regaining of British waters for British fishermen, but still nothing to compare with the glory days.

There was an interesting exhibition in the Passmore Edwards Gallery by the water's edge on the eastern end of Newlyn. There were paintings by well-known local artists Alice Mumford, Daphne McClure, Janet Treloar and Romy Tunstall-Behrens. Some varied styles by the ever-changing Wilhelmina Barnes-Graham were on their own in one corner, and a few by Patrick Heron were there too. It was a colourful and diverse show, and both enjoyed it. At the end they bought one of her strong semi-abstract water colours by Janet Treloar, partly as a memento of their visit, but mostly because they admired it. They returned to Penzance for a light lunch at the Queen's Hotel, then went down to the Gallery at Penlee House at the western end of the town, to see their permanent exhibition of Newlyn work. They particularly wanted to see the Jubilee Hat by Bourdillon, which belonged to friends of theirs and was on permanent loan to Penlee.

There were many places that Marina and Freddie wanted to visit, and their stay proved to be very short when they tried to fit everything in. They were determined to go down to Mousehole and look at the wonderfully old-fashioned fishing harbour, and to have stargazy pie either at the Old Coastguard, or the Harbour seafood restaurant. They also wanted to see a production at the Minack Theatre, depending upon what was showing and also on the weather.

All too soon, their time was up and they hadn't seen all the things that they had earmarked. That would just have to wait for another time. They could look forward to it, their lives lay ahead of them.

It was time to turn the Bentley to the east and then take it back up to the north and home to Derbyshire.

CHAPTER TWENTY-FIVE

After such a successful break and having discovered a deep love for each other, Freddie and Marina were married. Both were decisive people and neither saw any sense in delay. They had both made up their minds and it was time to get on and do it. So they did. Life had become immeasurably busier since their return from the Cornish adventure, and they had not been able to take time off or even have more than a long weekend's honeymoon. FH had been expanding at a prodigious rate and they had been hunting for and then had taken on more staff at every level. As the years sped by, the balance sheet was gaining strength and the profit and loss account showed at first less red ink, then eventually a healthy amount of black ink.

Grant Davenport had surfaced again from time to time, and tried to set up a meeting, but because of pressure of work, FH put him off with a promise of a meeting when life settled down again to a steadier running pace. After being given the run-around in this way a few times, this caused some anxiety within Guzzle and Grant had a few arguments with Mr Halkidopoulos who was fundamentally impatient and very much a man of action. The Chief Executive's view was, if it is potentially a goer, get going, it could only increase in value and create a possible demand in other unwelcome quarters if they did nothing. What were they waiting for? His message to Grant was if it's right for us, get out there and do a deal. Besides, Greeks like doing deals and this man was no exception.

Meanwhile FH grew and became better known in its market, and naturally being more visible and ostensibly more successful, the perceived value rose to reflect that. There was talk of getting a Stock Exchange listing, but at the moment none of the three principals wanted the hassle of public ownership. They feared, quite correctly, that such an action would limit their ability to run the company the way they wished and would impose any number of undesirable obligations on them. Besides, they now no longer needed to consider raising outside finance over and above the debt capital that their City banking associates, Siegel Dornhof, a

British subsidiary of the American bank AlleghenyBankCorp, had syndicated for them on very favourable terms. And so far, the interest payable had been reasonably painless.

Apart from the regular attempts from Grant Davenport to set up a meeting with the obvious intention of making a bid, there had been others who had done their homework and ferreted out FH for further attention. One was an institutionally funded buy-out-cum-predator merchant run by a red-blooded chancer called Jeremy Milton. He had contemplated an approach and had then made contact, but he had clearly decided that there was not much chance of a deal in the near future. Mr Milton preferred deals where a rescue was needed, and the target company would be in no position to resist. He liked only cheap and easy deals with big and under-used balance sheets, and soon went away. Another independent firm of M&A advisors had actually managed to get a meeting with Douglas. A couple of middle aged highly experienced and presentable Old Etonians had talked about possible acquisitions, but that had gone nowhere. Their firm was called Samuel Neale and Associates, and they certainly cut ice, but at FH there was at this moment no ice to cut.

When all seems organised, ship-shape, and well-oiled, and surrounding waters appear smooth, a pebble sometimes gets dropped into the calm of the pond, and confusion reigns for a bit. Freddie was reading the paper as he and Marina had their frugal breakfast. Neither was an avid newspaper reader and it wasn't unusual for them to miss a subject which might already have been raised in a preliminary, low key sort of a way. One such subject greeted Freddie as he worked his way idly through the pages of newsprint.

"Hey! Look at this. I know there have been rumblings for years and we haven't given it much thought but look here."

Freddie folded the paper and handed it to Marina.

"Good Lord. They've got long memories these Chinese, and they don't give up do they?"

The article that had caught Freddie's interest was the main story in the World News section of the paper. China was getting more aggressive with Taiwan. The article enumerated a collection of actions in which the Chinese were now threatening Taiwan with interference, even military engagement. They had declared the sea in the area as wholly Chinese, incorporating Formosa, Quemoy and Matsu, so that all those territories now lay within what China claimed as Chinese territorial waters. Huge numbers of Chinese Naval ships circled the area and the Chinese Air Force overflew all parts of those islands as and when they wished. Who could stop them? NATO was all talk and no teeth, America was totally disinclined to become involved again in any foreign conflicts, and there was no one else with either the power or the will to do anything about it. The civilised world was facing a fait accompli about which nothing would or could be done. The U.N. was as always equivocal and unable, unwilling even, to address the issue. It passed a bland resolution, which merely joined all the other bland resolutions, in the do-nothing bin. The world watched and prayed.

Markets were unhappy but had already discounted such an eventuality to a considerable extent. Indices fell, then rose again, only to see-saw up and down in a headless-chickenish way. Then gradually they settled again. They remembered Hong-Kong which had been a huge cause célèbre for a short time, then had been largely forgotten.

"What does this do to us, do you suppose?"

Freddie had no answer to this, he said,

"I have absolutely no idea. It could be anything from momentous to what-the-hell. I truly have no notion. I suspect that China will eventually grab Formosa without a shot being fired and the rest of the world will just take it lying down. That is what I think, what about you?"

"Well, much as I hate to agree, I can't see anything else happening. Poor old Taiwan, it's curtains I think."

As it turned out, that is exactly what happened. Markets trembled for a bit, then settled down, and the world forgot about Taiwan and its troubles. There was an underlying feeling that China itself would ultimately break down. You couldn't for ever rule by cruelty and terror, and with the continuing and ever faster development of communication, the Chinese population would not for an eternity put up with that form of rule. But how long would it take to fall apart? Jan Smuts in his diatribe on Empire had concluded that Empires generally lasted about two hundred and fifty years. That meant that China could last until twenty-one-fifty. We shall all be dead by then anyway. The paradox was that though it could take years to reach the point of disintegration, when that point was reached, change would happen overnight. Remember the fall of the Soviet Union.

As the dust settled, the international business world did what it always does. It adapted to the new circumstances and continued to do its best to placate China in the interests of selling them stuff and getting the Chinese to continue to make stuff for them. In short, the rest of the world ate humble pie and continued to thrive on that diet.

This development intensified further the move being made by western manufacturers to repatriate as much of their supply chains as they could, taking the work back from China. But that had little effect on China, and it would probably put up the cost of such products as motor cars.

There did turn out to be one advantage that arose out of the China fiasco. Other more obscure markets, many of them in the Far East, achieved greater significance to western trading companies. The need for reliable and comprehensive analysis of less obvious markets grew as a result, and this played nicely into the hands of FH.

The uncertainty arising from the Taiwan annexation eventually subsided. What had happened had happened, and the world continued to spin. Tomorrow continued to arrive on time. Once it became clear that the new situation was here to stay and things had, at least on the surface, stabilised, Grant Davenport made contact again. He was coming to London and would really appreciate a chance to meet Ms Slade-Knox, Mr Dominie and Mr Pitcurnow. He felt that there would be good sense in getting to know one another and he could tell them about his plans for the European market. He had constructed a few more entirely bogus and meaningless expressions but decided that what he had said was more than enough. He hoped that this time he would get a meeting. Mr Halkidopoulos would be mightily displeased if he failed again.

A date was made for the arrival of Grant Davenport, and it was intended that he should come to the office briefly and then they would repair to Douglas's home and have a meeting in his study. Douglas tidied the place up and made it look a bit more business-like before the day of the meeting.

Grant arrived on the train at Macclesfield in the morning and the plan was to take him to the office for a quick tour d'horizon, and then go over to Douglas's Old Rectory. Freddie was deputed to pick Grant up in his new Aston-Martin and bring him to the Stables. The new offices in the main house, Old Dale Park, already contained most of the staff, but the three principals had preferred to stay where they were before, so that is where Freddie took Grant before going over very briefly to the office in the Mansion which they went through like a dose of salts. There wasn't much to see and Freddie and the others didn't want to arouse suspicions by making a song and dance about it. Freddie took Grant up in the lift and they had no more than a cursory and very much a passing glimpse of one floor. No one in there showed the slightest interest, which was the intention.

Douglas and Marina took her Bentley over to the Old Rectory and soon after, Freddie drove up with Grant. The two specimens of England's best, the Aston and the Bentley, stood shining expensively in the sun to one side of the entrance, pointing outwards.

Douglas offered elderflower spritzers all around and they sat at the Sheraton table. He rang a bell and his man appeared. Douglas said,

"I thought we would have a light lunch, then we can discuss whatever Grant would like to bring up. We can of course tell you whatever you would like to know about Far Horizons, then we'll see where all that takes us. One of us will get you back into Macclesfield for the train back to London."

Niceties were paraded briefly by all parties, nobody wishing to be thought to be keen on digging into the serious stuff too soon. Grant had discovered that you didn't get down to business in too much of a hurry in this country, you could easily weaken your position by doing that, but you could also damage your standing by hanging back too much. So far so good. This stage was a bit like dogs sniffing each other's bottoms.

Douglas spoke,

"Now, Grant, tell us if you would what Guzzle's plans are for the future over here. Since leaving the E. U. this country is now really motoring, so I expect you have some master plan up your sleeve."

"We at Guzzle see Europe and the U. K. as a great market opportunity, and it is my job to try and move things along a bit. That's why I am over here, and I must say, I am impressed with what I have seen. The U. K. particularly has really got its skates on."

"That is exactly how we see it. Not so long ago we were a tiny new boy on the block, now we are making plenty of waves. This year our gross take will be forty-eight percent up on last year and we are now very much a known quantity. As always we are on the hunt for good people. Right now, I would say that is our greatest task. By no means an impossibility, but it requires constant hard work, and that's what we give it."

This kind of scene setting continued for some time, Grant trying his hardest to judge his moment. Finally, after much circular conversation, he spoke.

"I wonder, has it ever occurred to you that some form of liaison with a larger player might speed you better on your way?"

Freddie came in with,

"You know, we have been at such full stretch getting ourselves to where we are today that we haven't considered that."

Grant said,

"Well, there might be huge benefits to be gained by having the worldwide reach of a major player, like for example Guzzle. The chance to get further in less time could be very beneficial."

Marina had the thought that she would love just to say,

"OK then how much?"

But she didn't. She ran her fingers through her immaculate hair and folded her hands in her lap and said nothing. Douglas spoke.

"Tell me Grant, I'm not sure I understood that, could you perhaps explain it for us?"

"I'm thinking that the combination of what we do and what you do seems to me to be very complementary. You would take us into new areas of activity and we would take you into new markets."

It was now Douglas's turn to think, "Go on, tell us, how much?" But he didn't say anything for a moment. An interval of silence never did any harm. Make the other side sweat a bit. Douglas said,

"How are your glasses doing? Can I fill you up?"

Hands went up declining. Grant returned to the charge, it was now or never with these tricky monkeys.

"We've given this a lot of thought at Guzzle. We think there is the chance of a very synergistic relationship between our two companies, and I would like to get your reaction to how you think we might exploit this opportunity."

"We wouldn't turn our backs on opportunities, after all, that's how we got here, and I've already told you what our historical rate of growth has been. I haven't yet alluded to what we can already see for next year. We have quite a good idea of our medium-term order potential, our estimates have been comfortably exceeded these last four years. I see no problem in telling you that for the next fiscal year we would be surprised if our revenues didn't beat this current year's income by very nearly one hundred percent. We are fortunate to have the kind of close relationship with our major customers that gives us a clear idea of where they are going and therefore where we may expect to go with them."

"Impressive stuff. That's the world we both operate in, I guess. Do you have a particularly large population of major customers, are we talking fifty? A hundred? More?"

"Without giving away state secrets, we are comfortably into the high hundreds and rising. That is our future, and we are no slouches there, thanks to Marina and her capable crew."

"I see, that's good, very good. I am very encouraged by that, there is clearly a lot that we could accomplish together. Look, I want to tell you in strict confidence that we at Guzzle have earmarked FH as a very desirable partner. I am here with the authorisation and encouragement of Mr Halkidopoulos to discuss with you the possibility of combining our joint and substantial potentialities."

None of the three showed any inclination to be the one to answer this, so silence ensued. Then Douglas spoke,

"I think what you are skating around is the subject of an acquisition of FH by Guzzle. For the avoidance of doubt, am I right?"

Freddie and Marina gave an undetectable sigh of relief. Now we know where we are. Grant certainly likes to go round in circles, but now it's out on the table. His move.

Grant paused and looked at each of them in turn.

"I guess that's the size of it, yes. It would be a great pleasure for Guzzle to do business with FH, and yes, we are in a mood to make such an acquisition. How does that strike you?"

CHAPTER TWENTY-SIX

The meeting with Grant Davenport came swiftly to an end, Douglas having said,

"Grant, thank you for that. We would like to give this some thought, but I think I speak for the three of us when I say that we can all see the logic of your approach and we shall take that into account and give it serious thought this evening. If you felt it worthwhile, I would like to suggest that you postpone your trip back to London and we reconvene in the morning. We'll make a booking for you and have you run in and out of Macclesfield. How would it suit you to be back here at nine o'clock in the morning tomorrow, and we can see whether there is enough common ground to go further?"

"Thank you, just let me check my messages, I can see no reason not to do as you say."

Grant tapped his smart phone into action and confirmed that the morning was fine.

Douglas's man drove Grant to his hotel in the Porsche, and the three of them sat back and pondered the new situation.

Marina spoke first,

"I don't know about you, but I think this sounds good so far. Knowing what these people are like, though, we must get a confidentiality agreement with real teeth before showing them anything. I vote we take this seriously."

Freddie came in with,

"No harm in hearing him out. I think we can take it that this is serious, they've been at us for quite a time. What do you think Douglas?"

"I say never look a gift horse in the mouth; you don't know what the future may bring, and opportunities come and they go. I sense that Guzzle will pay handsomely for this, they've had their eyes on it for long enough. And I absolutely agree about the confidentiality thing, you can't be too careful, particularly with Americans, and God knows, there's a Greek at the middle of this one. Remember Virgil's 'Quidquid id est, timeo Danaos et dona ferentis'? I agree with the wise old Roman, and the confidentiality letter must be bristling with teeth."

Freddie felt that at this moment he should say something about the debt funding which Douglas and Marina had put up for the Charter deal, without which there would have been no play.

"You two, I just want to say first of all how grateful I am to you for the debt you put up earlier to make the Charter deal run. It is thanks to you two that I could match your contributions to getting Far Horizons up to this stage at this time. And I want to thank you for funding this whole thing at the very beginning. Just so you both know and hear it from me now."

"Thanks, Freddie. We wouldn't have done any of this, or the Charter deal, without you. There should be a decent pay-off here for us all."

There followed a discussion during which they tried to agree a ballpark figure that they would be pleased to take. None of them would do the actual negotiating, that would be done by James Struther who was head of Corporate Finance at Siegel Dornhof and specialised in Mergers and Acquisitions. He would be ably assisted by Noel Lincoln. The three only wanted to see where they put the value themselves, just to know that they were on the right lines. All the face-to-face stuff would be done by the Merchant Bankers. The three Partners would adopt a lofty and silent position over the whole thing.

A Magnum of Veuve Clicquot met its glorious end after they had talked the thing through. They all agreed that none of them would say anything of any substance in the morning, the sole purpose was to leave Grant knowing that a deal would be possible and that the next move must be his. Nothing more. FH would of course co-operate with Guzzle's due diligence exercise and they would be happy to let one of the big six accountancy firms in to do an investigation once a deal had been agreed in principle. There would be a time limit on all of this, ideally three months, by which time there should either be a binding heads of agreement or a parting of the ways.

Marina and Freddie returned to her home and went into the kitchen. Marina took off her bra because the underwires were digging into her, and immediately put on her apron. She gave Freddie a no-you-don't look and said,

"I don't know about you, but I could kill scrambled eggs."

"Me too. Would you like me to do it? That's one of the things I do quite well."

"No, I would not. There are other things you do better, and I think we need to celebrate later with a damned good fuck."

Grant returned on the dot of nine o'clock.

Douglas welcomed him back with the words,

"Thanks for coming back. We are prepared to give you a certain amount of time to come back to us with your proposals in principle. If you get to the stage of doing due diligence we would be delighted to give you all the help you and your accountants might need. I take it you would be using one of the big six?"

"We would use Bryce Winterton Kroupah. And I think I can say that we would certainly like to take this further. To that end I will get the outline of a proposal out to you during the next working week. There will of course be no final details on value at this stage, but we can make it clear what the ballpark figure is. Then if we agree, we would want to get on with due diligence straight away, and then get the accountants' report under way. There is no point in delaying."

"If we agree to the tenor of your proposals, we would need to get you to enter into a confidentiality agreement for say three months during which time you would have exclusivity, and our lawyers will get onto that if we get that far."

"Sounds good to me."

Grant returned to the Valley feeling that he had done a good job, the Gods were smiling on him. Mr Halkidopoulos was visibly excited.

"Well done Grant, we'll have these Limeys. Go to it, no point in delaying. Get back to them straight away and give them the feeling that they are going to do well out of this. No commitment mind, but rich enough to get them on the hook. We can, and probably will, trim later when we get Bryce's accountants' report. That will be the time for the short strokes. You just get them well and truly hooked, OK?"

Douglas rang Siegel Dornhof and spoke to James Struther.

"James, the business with Guzzle I mentioned to you the other day. It looks as though we might be getting somewhere. Will you stand by to represent us? Could be quite soon, we intend giving them three months from receipt of their letter to reach a Heads and will you please put together a good tough confidentiality agreement? Their chief honcho is a Greek! They will be back with an expression of interest next week, and after that it will dictate its own pace. They will be using Bryce to do the accountants' report and they will have a team of their own people doing due diligence. Their lawyers will be Scravitz and Spears, you've dealt with them before haven't you? Typical New York firm. We shall be using Sleeman Goodhart and Meyer, Bob Strindberg. You know him too, don't you?"

"I do. You get to know most of them in this business. Scravitz can be tiresome. Very sharp pencils and the New York ethic writ large. Never mind, our team is pretty good so I'm not worried."

"OK James, we'll keep you posted. I think this may fly."

Meanwhile, Grant was back in the Valley and working out just what he should say in his letter. He decided that there was no point in trying to be specific in telling FH what their value might roughly be. He decided that the best thing at this stage would be to refer to a value in the high hundreds of millions with the possibility of an order of magnitude more should facts arise beyond their present expectations. He finished off by saying that the value that Guzzle would put on the business would be substantially more than any competitor could afford, because of the obvious and proven compatibility and complementary nature of the two businesses. He ran his letter past Mr Halkidopoulos who said,

"That should do it. You might want to sweeten it a bit, but for Heaven's sake don't actually say any more. Just give it to them nice and enticing. Lure them on a bit, but I leave that to you. You know what you are doing."

CHAPTER TWENTY-SEVEN

After much to-ing and fro-ing between the New York lawyers Scravitz and the City lawyers Sleeman, which had given rise to much spilling of red ink, the time was right to have a meeting in Sleeman's office in Bishopsgate to examine the drafting of the documents which would seal the deal. The first principle was that any and all legal matters would be governed by English law.

The value placed on the business by Guzzle had come in at a figure which exceeded that postulated amongst themselves by the three partners. Noughts had flown around like a new hatch of flies in a stuffy warm bedroom. However, they knew that there was still the interpretation of the accountants report to discuss, and all knew that this would be the time when the negative stuff would be introduced and the final horse-trading would get under way.

There had also been a good deal of discussion about warranties and indemnities. James Struther at Siegels had played hardball over this issue.

"It is not my client's intention to sign warranties or indemnities, your accountant's report and your due diligence will surely cover that."

Scravitz's M&A partner, Abel Goldstein, had come back with,

"My clients, on my advice, would be forced to review the whole deal if we couldn't be reassured by the knowledge that your clients were at risk if the facts or the performance were to differ significantly from what they had told us. That means warranties and indemnities."

"Should this deal go ahead, your clients will be in charge and ours will be substantially out of the picture. Our clients cannot be expected to underwrite the forecasts that they have made in good faith and against a backdrop of having been conservative in the past and having exceeded those forecasts in each of the last five years, when they no longer play any part in the running of the new company. That put simply would not be equitable."

"We'll leave the forecasts for the moment. On the subject of warranties, it would not be equitable if my clients were forced to pay the price of past misdemeanours by your clients. Hence the importance of the warranting of the information you have provided."

"Past performance will be fully covered by Bryce's report and we have already passed to them confirmatory correspondence with the UK tax authorities to the effect that all taxes have been paid and that we are not under any kind of investigation. Of course after you own the company, tax affairs will be your concern, but there is nothing in the past or at this time which could give rise to anything that you might wish to avoid."

The accountants report had not revealed anything of substance upon which Guzzle could hang a price renegotiation. That didn't stop them from trying, and the unmistakable smell of a Greek at work was apparent to the partners. What was needed was patience and persistence. When warranties and indemnities had looked like a terminal barrier to completion, Grant had been in touch with Mr Halkidopoulos.

"Mr Halkidopoulos, I am having no luck over these warranties and indemnities, what do you want me to do?"

"What kind of trouble?"

"Won't sign kind of trouble."

"What assurances have they given us? Any?"

"Things like confirmation from the Revenue in the UK that they're not on their tails and they don't owe any back tax. Good stuff from their banks, that's about it really."

"OK Grant. Fuck this. We'll go with that. Just get it done now, OK?"

"It will be done, Mr Halkidopoulos."

And it was, but first the pleasurable ritual had to be gone through of agreeing the final price to go in the documents. At this moment there were only black footballs in the drafts where real figures would eventually appear.

Mr Halkidopoulos, being familiar with the regular buying and selling of ships upon which his country thrived, stuck his oar in. He wanted and got daily updates from Grant on the progress in that direction. The banking advisors had born the load of most of the horse trading, but Grant, on Mr Halkidopoulos's instructions, had intervened as often as he was told to do so, and sometimes on his own initiative. They were nearly there, but a meeting had been set up in the City to finalise the thing before a completion meeting which was scheduled to follow soon after.

Grant and the partners of EH had been shown into Siegel Dornhof's City conference room under the chairmanship of James Struther with his assistant Noel Lincoln beside him. Trimble Oppenheimer of Grabel Black, New York investment bankers, were representing Guzzle. Trimble was assisted by a keen young man, Isaac Bloom, who obviously saw this deal as his chance to make a mark and advance his quest ultimately to run the whole show. James made a mental note to keep Isaac talking if things got sticky. People like that can't keep their mouths shut and you can discover a lot that way. James was well aware of the power of silence and part of his plan was to deploy a lot of it. He had briefed Noel to that effect. The purpose of this meeting was to tie up all the loose ends, which meant finally agree the exact price and means of payment. All else was done and ready to go.

The question of method of payment came up again. EH had said that it would prefer an all cash deal. They didn't show much enthusiasm for a share exchange, even though, as Trimble Oppenheimer had argued, you could make a good case for holding some Guzzle paper. It was finally agreed that the FH shareholders would accept ten percent in paper, the rest in cash. To achieve that, Grabel Black would almost certainly have to conduct a placement of a large amount of Guzzle stock. They would probably choose to spread it amongst the Trusts they managed and let it out slowly and in a controlled manner to the market over a period which they would control. Too much too soon would damage the price. None of this concerned the EH shareholders who enjoyed a brief glimpse of Grabel Black advising their client. That soon stopped and Guzzle agreed the requested cash to paper ratio of ten to ninety. The question of the final price never became a burning disagreement. The meeting witnessed agreement growing without anybody's direct intervention. This was most unusual. It led the three partners to wonder whether they had agreed too soon and could have got more. They all concluded independently that the price was quite enough, and preparations were put in hand to set up the completion meeting in Sleeman Goodhart and Meyer's office early the following week. As part of the agreement, the partners were to remain as consultants, for which they would be paid handsomely, for three years. They accepted this request, but each knew that the most likely outcome would be a falling out and a suit for compensation on the grounds of constructive dismissal. At this moment none of that bothered them in the slightest.

Three exhausted but very happy people returned on the train to Macclesfield. They all slept on the way, there was nothing more to be said, and each was glad of a pause and a rest.

They all went home and first had a bite of whatever they could find in the fridge, then went gratefully to bed. The impact of what they had agreed had not yet sunk in fully with any of them. Of course, each of them understood perfectly what had happened, but the shot of full realisation had not yet reached the brain. Soon it would.

After Freddie had eaten a cheese and Branston sandwich and washed it down with a can of Jumping Bean ale, he turned to Marina who was just finishing some smoked salmon and thin brown bread with a glass of Cava.

"I'm done for. But done for in a marvellous way, how about you?"

"Barely alive, but excited beyond measure. No fucking tonight, but let's screw ourselves into next week tomorrow morning."

They both felt exhausted by the thought and went peacefully to bed and deep sleep.

Marina went instantly to sleep and the still awake Freddie heard her laugh. She later told him that she had had a dream in which she kept giving black eyes to Grant Davenport. Every time she hit him an eye went black, and then she did it again and again and again. The laughter did not wake her up, and she slept on. After tossing and turning, Freddie escaped into the most profound slumber. Not until nearly nine o'clock did they wake fully. Both remembered the promise of the evening before, and the next thirty-five minutes were memorably athletic.

Douglas woke at five past eight and pushed his man out of the other side of the bed.

"I've got good news; I'm putting your wages up. And here's the key to a new BMW. It's yours, you'll find it locked in the far garage. With my love."

He turned over, finally able to relish openly and fully the realisation of what the three of them had achieved.

The completion meeting took place and the three partners all made an unbelievable amount of money, on top of what they had all made before. When the meeting was over, they repaired to Valentino's Bar in Dean Street and put away a magnum of Bollinger, then went to the three Michelin star restaurant, The Jolly Brexiteer in Wardour Street, and had a slap-up dinner before going to the Savoy for a luxuriously comfortable night.

Douglas was on his own, Freddie and Marina continued the celebration until neither could move even their little finger.

Life opened up for these three fortunate people and their Far Horizons now stretched into infinity.

EPILOGUE

"Did you ever imagine anything like this would happen, making inhuman amounts of money, I mean?"

"I did, actually, you know how a simple teenage boy can dream up all sorts of things, and I always felt that something extraordinary would happen. I had always felt an outsider you see."

"I was just an English country girl who got bored and went to America to see what it was like. I was lucky, I had always loved maths and felt at home in my own little world of numbers where nobody could get at me."

"That's pretty much how I felt too."

"Then events seemed to take over and I just got swept along. I still don't really know how it all happened."

"Me too. But my private world of figures and equations provided me with impetus which took me into all this. You got there first, and without you and dear old Douglas, I would be stacking shelves and doing crosswords between cuddling the cat and boiling up baked beans."

Marina looked at him indulgently and laughed out loud.

"I tried awfully hard not to fall in love with you, did you know that?"

"I can't say I did. I was unbelievably shy about letting you see what I really thought, so I tried to be cool and not give anything away. You had me hooked from the time of that trip to the Valley all those years ago. But I was scared that you wouldn't look at a five foot nothing little runt like me."

"And now you're my little runt!"

"And I've got a couple of inches over you now,"

Said with a little admixture of pride.

"Not when I put my heels on you haven't."

It was a sunny summer evening and they were sitting on the terrace at Sterndale Manor, the house in the Peaks which they had bought together some years back, after the money had rolled in. Freddie's ambition had finally been realised. Sterndale had a moat. The house was a stone built Georgian structure, noted by

Pevsner for its fenestration and its proportions. Even the word perfection had been used by the Great Man. The house stood plumb in the middle of a five hundred acre home farm, which provided a little, but insignificant amount towards the upkeep of the house. It was unashamedly a hobby farm and was tenanted to a gentleman farmer, an amateur horticulturalist who also specialised in rare breeds and was wedded to the principle of providing appropriate environments for the varied wildlife which resided there. His name was Saul Thwaites and his wife was Betty.

The union between Freddie and Marina had produced no children, and the outlook in that respect was unpromising. Marina had endured three pregnancies of which none had been successful. She had had three miscarriages at between two and three months. The aftermath had been agonising for Marina and for Freddie. It seemed to both of them to be a pity not to have a new generation with whom to share their great good fortune. Neither wished, however, to adopt. They both felt that that could create more problems in the future than it solved in the present. Much discussion went on between them about how to make the best and most useful future with the resources that they now had, although no final answer to the conundrum had yet surfaced. Paradoxically, they were both inclining to the belief that the most provident way to help the human race to live within its means and in harmony with nature, was to promote birth control in third world countries. This had always presented a thankless task and an unsuccessful outcome. Close to this thought was a desire to improve the lot of women in those same places and to prevent such barbaric ongoing atrocities as female genital mutilation. The more they thought about these problems, the more they felt that they must do something about them. They were doing this with their eyes open, they knew how counter cultural these endeavours would be in a wide number of countries, but were in no way deterred from examining ways to alleviate these ills as a result of that knowledge. They were well aware of the fact that their enormous wealth was insignificantly small when it came to trying to solve problems like those that they had identified. The answer must include a way of tying in some real heavy weight help in order to make progress in these identified areas.

Government co-operation must be gained if any advances were to be made. That meant help from a number of governments, not just ours. Even perhaps the United Nations, but maybe that organisation represented too much those very places where these ills were most practised.

Thus, by 2028 was born the Slade Pitcurnow Initiative, funded by these two fine and public-spirited citizens. Its purpose was to fight for women's wellbeing and to contribute towards the full freedom of them in oppressed third world countries, and to promote and fund birth control in those same areas. To that end, the Board of Control consisted of British ex-Ambassadors from Paris, Washington, Moscow, South Africa and Kenya. Many of the support staff were from the British and American military and from medical research teams at leading international hospitals, augmented by two owners of large public relations firms with experience of working in the relevant countries. The total of the Initiative's employees and board was thirty-six souls. Marina and Freddie were supernumerary special advisers and were not included in that number.

The beginning was extremely promising, and the august board made good progress in putting their case before the right people in the major developed countries, which were their main target for support. While actual tangible forward movement in the affected countries remained hard to detect, the developed countries with one or two exceptions, all made the right noises. In a small peripheral part of deepest Congo, there was what appeared to be some early success. Figures were published by the regional governor, a General Brasshat Ogawalu, to the effect that his state of Zenzawele, a region of Congo, was applying remedies advocated by the Slade Pitcurnow Initiative, in which his government had great faith. So far so good, this was a promising and unexpected start.

It was not long before news came out of Zenzawele that it had seceded from the Congo. Its internal army, hitherto of unknown size and effectiveness, had supported the movement as well as the creation of a new independent state of the same name. Gradually information surfaced to the effect that this army, which turned out to be made up of fifty thousand well trained but semi free-booting troops, was led by an ex-SAS sergeant of unknown name, referred to as General Jehoshaphat. The new president of the new state was none other than Generalissimo Brasshat Ogawalu. Thinking back to the dreadful experiences under Mugabe in Zimbabwe, opinion was divided as to whether this was a good thing or a disaster waiting to happen. It was in fact a disaster and nobody had to wait long to make that discovery. Ogawalu's first action was to raise the pay of the army, and to rename it The Civilisation and Freedom Corps. Further, he introduced the scarlet uniforms of the Foot Guards including their bearskins for smart occasions, of which he intended there should be many. Legend had it that he had ordered a State Coach based on the design of the Gold State Coach used by the Queen, Thankfully it had been simplified and lightened from the four tons of the original, and was to be drawn by five Zenzawele Greys in a formation of three leading horses abreast followed by a pair. The result of this design change was that the new vehicle appeared to owe more to Walt Disney that to Her Majesty. It was being built in secret by a small coachbuilding firm that normally restored vintage cars, in Wiltshire, called Anything on Wheels, run by an ex-Mulliner employee with a waxed moustache and a goatee beard. It was said that he had served as a sergeant in R.E.M.E. at Fallingbostel, and the coach displayed small glimpses of a battle tank in its design.

Ogawalu had clearly read and absorbed Mugabe's book, "how to get what you want and fool the world". He got what he thought he wanted, but this time the world was not fooled. Recognition was either denied or withdrawn, sanctions came next and their bite was soon felt. None of this, however had any effect on The People's Democratic Commonwealth of Zenzawele. Life, seasoned with death, prevailed. Objection and demonstration were met with gunfire, and all the ambitions of Slade Pitcurnow were dashed. Such news as leaked out of that inferno stated that women had been raped by the thousand and treatment of them went back to how it was before the stone age. No journalists were allowed into the country and every effort to contain news was made. Those pressmen and women who were there when the disaster struck were locked up in solitary confinement, starved and beaten. It was believed that most had already died and many had been killed. Even the floppy political left was forced to recognise the extent of the misfortune and the headlong fall of a country which was already in terminal decline before its declaration of independence from the Congo. It didn't pay to go into the story of the Congo itself either. The whole of that land had belonged personally to King Leopold II of the Belgians who had kept it as his private country estate and his own secret domain in which brutality was the main blood sport. It had never recovered from that formative and shaming experience.

The story did not end with Zenzawele. Other countries in the dark continent tried copycat coups, but so far none had succeeded. The effect of that, however, was to take the eye off the main points of the Slade Pitcurnow Initiative in trying to improve the lot of those unfortunate nations. It was a grave setback. Nothing for it but to renew efforts with developed countries and return to the charge as opportunity arose. At the moment, though, all looked dead or dying.

Time passed and the fortunes of the Initiative's target countries rose and fell with the tide of fate. Peace in one would point relentlessly to conflict in another, and corruption was unstoppable. SPI had learnt, as had most of the civilised world, that money should never be used directly with the rulers of these rogue places. All financial support was arranged with reliable external bodies from countries which obeyed the rule of law and were civilised. These institutions would be paid directly, nothing going through the channels of the beneficiary states. But that didn't always work. There was enough of the folding stuff floating around through drug dealing and other nefarious activities, to say nothing of funds from non-compliant countries. This provided more than adequate slush money for such as Generalissimo Brasshat Ogawalu, President of The People's Democratic Commonwealth of Zenzawele. These world-scale large stashes resided in places like Switzerland. Behind a façade of quiet responsibility, the gnomes were still good for a bit of secrecy in special cases. Special cases included presidents of generously cash-flooded countries like Zenzawele. The grandest of Mercedes-Benz cars flowed in and the President's Peace Force One was the latest version of the Grumman Gulfstream private business jet. Notably its flight attendants were all tall slim sexy white girls. The pilots were Zenzawelians trained at Biggin Hill in England on Hawk trainers and latterly on the spare Gulfstream which Zenzawele kept there in reserve.

Freddie and Marina had reduced their involvement in Far Horizons. Having sold out to Guzzle, the company's ambitions had increased dramatically and had also veered away from what these two founders had envisaged. Their time could now be devoted entirely to the Initiative and would not be needed by FH, or rather Guzzle FH, other than in a way that was more ceremonial than real. The advisory fees came in handy, the Initiative could use every penny that went its way.

Sterndale Manor had begun to mature most satisfactorily. Trees were growing apace, the gardens had responded magnificently to the attentions of Saul Thwaites, a graduate of Bristol University who had read Engineering, and had come into enough of a small fortune to remove the necessity to compete for ever more lucrative jobs. He could live comfortably on his private income, but his greatest love was horticulture as well as the husbandry of the Sterndale Home Farm. He had married Betty, a Bristol girl whose family were very well-known garden lovers and proprietors in Somerset and the West Country, and she had taken the graft well. She loved the tending of plants and the intellectual side of communing with nature. These two had leased the Dower House, a small Georgian beauty, also noticed and given a nod by Pevsner, a mile or so away from the Manor. They had taken the large garden in hand, and this, together with a partnership arrangement for the farm, was where they augmented their respectable but not excessive corn. This gave pleasure to Marina and Freddie, both of whom were quite happy to work in the garden on rare occasions. This they did under the instruction and orders of the Thwaiteses, by happy and mutual agreement. Betty Thwaites had turned out to be a more than respectable painter in oils, too.

Life continued in busy vein for the Pitcurnows. They had come to accept the fact that children were a sad improbability, and anyway, they found themselves so busy on the Initiative that there wasn't time to mope about this sad state of affairs.

Marina had spoken to an old San Francisco friend, Sal, the wife of a man, Al, she had worked with. That couple had been in England for the inside of a week, having toured France,

Germany, Italy, and the Low Countries in the previous week. Honestly, thought Marina, how on earth can you see anything beyond the inside of a plane, a train, or a car in that time? The Americans were like that, but these people had taken the trouble before setting sail for Europe to get in touch again with Marina and make a date for a one-night visit on their way from Stratford to Edinburgh. All this mention of mindless rapid travel made Marina feel tired. Not much made Marina feel tired, but this did.

When Sal and Al finally made it, Marina and Sal sat over a spritzer in the garden late in the afternoon, while Freddie and Al were walking the farm. Marina unusually let her hair down. This was in response to a question from her old Californian friend Sally-Gaye Dupont, Allington's wife, about children. Did Marina want some?

"Well, I must tell you, we haven't had much luck there. I have lost three in fairly quick succession, so we are a bit wary of trying again."

"I must tell you then. There is a new thing on the market in the States. We call it Baby Glue. They've given it some unpronounceable medical name, but I can e-mail it to you if you like. It is apparently a wonder worker and could be your answer. Far and away the best of all these magic things they keep inventing. I know from the experience of friends that this one does work."

"Oh, would you? I feel it is such a pity not to have any little ones, but you play the hand you are dealt, don't you? And we have come to think we didn't have the right constitution or something. Yes, I would be grateful if you could let me know."

"If I get it on Google when I go up to change, then I can give it to you at supper time. If you can't get it here, I can always get it for you Stateside."

"I'd really appreciate that. You never know, it may just work for me too. I am definitely game to give it a go, but I think I'll keep it a secret until we know. I don't want to go raising hopes only to see them dashed again, and I know Freddie would be over the moon if we managed to produce a little person."

Betty Thwaites had proved to be a willing helper in the kitchen when Marina was short-handed and needed a little help. She had turned out to be a more than competent cook too.

Nothing exotic, but decidedly north of Nursery. She had made a beef Wellington for this evening - Marina wanted to show Sal and Al proper English roast beef. Betty had also made a golden syrup pudding which was distinctly nursery. Betty and Marina felt sure the visitors would be pleased, knowing that they wouldn't get it anywhere else unless they went to Rules in Covent Garden. Betty was an entertaining companion to have around, she was an intelligent girl and she had an enticing sense of fun. The rest of the meal was fruit, cheese, and good coffee. Marina couldn't stand bad weak coffee, and Freddie wouldn't touch it either. The absolute limit was Instant.

After supper they all went into the drawing room, and as they walked through, Sal gave Marina a tiny scrap of paper on which she had written in her round and looped educated American-lady handwriting. It said simply and slightly haltingly given the complexity of the words, Baby Glue. Teremorolin. Made by Amphigiatrevo Corporation, Rancho Cucamonga, California. Marina pocketed it and they all went in and sat in comfortable chairs.

Conversation was predictably banal. The girls had a fair bit of catching up to do, which meant nothing to Freddie. He was heavily engaged with Al in conversation which from what she overheard, Marina recognised to be mostly about cars and motor bikes. She distinctly heard the words Harley-Davidson and knew she needn't worry about Freddie.

The next morning at eight o'clock the Duponts left for Edinburgh. Two days later Marina received a post card from Scotland ending with the words, good luck.

Freddie asked why they'd wished us good luck. Was it a normal American greeting or a jolly parting shot?

Marina looked at him with a forced casualness, having decided to say nothing about Baby Glue.

"No, I've no idea why, just friendly I think. I've always liked those two."

A year later, Augustus Frederick Pitcurnow was born, a strapping nine pounds two ounces, and now that Marina had got the hang of things, Cordelia May Pitcurnow followed close on the little boy's heels.

Ingram Content Group UK Ltd.
Milton Keynes UK
UKHW021951130323
418485UK00014B/853

9 781915 889355